Arthur T. Vanderbilt II

# Gardening in Eden

*The Joys of*
*Planning*
*and*
*Tending a*
*Garden*

Simon & Schuster

New York  London  Toronto  Sydney  Singapore

SIMON & SCHUSTER
Rockefeller Center
1230 Avenue of the Americas
New York, NY 10020

SIMON & SCHUSTER and colophon are registered
trademarks of Simon & Schuster, Inc.

For information about special discounts for bulk purchases,
please contact Simon & Schuster Special Sales:
1-800-456-6798 or business@simonandschuster.com

*Illustrations copyright © 2003 by Alexis Seabrook*
*Designed by Amy Hill*

Manufactured in the United States of America

1   3   5   7   9   10   8   6   4   2

Library of Congress Cataloging-in-Publication Data
Vanderbilt, Arthur T.
Gardening in Eden : the joys of planning and tending a garden /
Arthur T. Vanderbilt II.
p. cm.
1. Landscape gardening. I. Title.
SB473 .V33 2003
635.9—dc21      2002036680
ISBN 0-7432-4180-0

*To Michael Korda*

There is nowhere recorded a simple and irrepressible satisfaction with the gift of life.

—Henry David Thoreau

The Sun will not rise, or set, without my notice, and thanks.

—Winslow Homer

The students of an enlightened monk walked up to him as he was working in his garden and asked, "If you knew you had only fifteen minutes left to live, what would you do, Master?" The monk smiled, said, "This" and went back to his gardening.

—from Bernie S. Siegel, M.D.
*Prescriptions for Living*

# CONTENTS

# Gardening in Eden

# PREFACE

I WONDER if a high school or college student reading *Walden* can know what Thoreau meant when he said, "I have travelled a good deal in Concord." I'm certain I didn't. When we're young, the world is elsewhere. Years ago the sons and daughters of the privileged were sent on the Grand Tour, an exploration of the exotic capitals of Europe. Today's Huck Finns, with a backpack and some ingenuity, can find themselves in the most far-flung outposts of the globe.

But somewhere along the way, sometime in our lives, I think we begin to sense that the world is not somewhere else. It is, in fact, in Concord. It is wherever we are.

Indeed, Thoreau's insight has been recognized by some of the greatest travel writers after years of wandering the world. "This," wrote Robert Louis Stevenson, "is one of the lessons of travel—that some of the strangest races dwell next door to you at home." Paul Theroux noted, "I have come to believe that travel is mostly in the mind. . . . The whole point of travel is discovery, and few experiences can match the satisfaction of . . . an extraordinary discovery near home." For Jan Morris, "the truest truths are small ones, to be discovered wherever you are. If I could have my time over again, I think I would choose to roam only my own small patch of country—my bro, as we say in Wales. Instead of exploring continents and empires, I would investigate ever more intensely our modest fields, hills and villages; rather than wild beasts of Africa, I would watch the herons on the river, the frogs in the pond." Thoreau was right, of course: there's no need for tours and cruises, no need to plan safaris or trips of adventure and discovery. It's all happening right here, right where you are.

Perhaps gardeners become ardent gardeners when they begin to feel this. I'm amazed, now, what little regard I gave the property when I moved into my home twenty-five years ago. If the grass was reasonably green and reasonably trim, well, that was pretty much the beginning and end of my thoughts about landscaping. I don't even remember walking around the property much, small as it is—less than a half acre—and certainly I never ventured into the woodland parcel choked knee-high with weeds and tangled in vines and brambles and briers and poison ivy. I had no grand vision of how landscaping might transform this lot; indeed, I had no vision at all. The extent of my gardening was a burst of enthusiasm each spring when I planted the small terrace garden, then watched in deepening resignation as, by midsummer, the plants and flowers had withered or keeled over, disappeared, become deformed or died.

Now, I have no doubt that a professional landscape architect could have stopped over on a Saturday morning, looked around, sketched out a plan, and a very good one at that, and with the infusion of enough money, the plan could have been well executed within a week or two. But the joy of gardening is in doing it yourself, in devising a plan or parts of a plan, reflecting on it, refining it as you go along, revising it, fine-tuning it, figuring out, season by season, how the pieces fit together, what works well together, what has absolutely no interest in living on your property and what is quite happy there. And in this long process of trial and error, of great plans laid and gone awry, of crushing defeats and tiny victories, a sense of wonder awakens and you begin to realize you are traveling in Concord. Season to season, year by year, grows an amazement, an appreciation, of just how extraordinary is this tiny sliver of the earth and all that is happening on it.

The gardens of which I write are around my home in northern New Jersey, on a fairly typical suburban lot, but could just as easily be in Concord or anywhere. I will say this: my property does have unusual bones. I call them good bones, though others might not be so charitable. It's on the side of a ridge, and with the steep configuration of the land, the neighbors on three sides don't feel close, and on the fourth side, which overlooks a wildlife reservation, the out-look stretches for miles. The rolling topography allows for stone walls and steps and paths that lead to different vistas, elements that may not work as well on a perfectly flat parcel of land. On the other hand, the soil on the ridge is thin and poor, and any hole deep enough to plant a self-respecting perennial necessitates the extraction of rock, and the old oaks dapple the sunlight for most of the day.

But this is what I have and where I garden, and now not a day goes by, early morning, that I don't wander around to see what's happening before I go to work; not an evening, if there's still light, when I don't check to find out what I've missed. And a weekend when the weather or commitments prevent a good amount of work in the garden feels like a weekend wasted and lost forever.

Is mine an award-winning garden? Pictured in gardening

magazines and books? The destination of garden tours? No. Not yet, at least. The more I wander around the gardens, the more new ideas I have, and with each one there's more I want to do. Maybe by next year I'll get it just the way I want it. Or the year after that.

But let me show you around now.

# Waiting Weather

# I

DARK.

Dreary.

January days.

Days of leaden skies, of sleet and snow flurries, day after day, depressing days of winter. Layers of heavy woolen clouds blanket days without sunlight, murky gray days from morning until late afternoon when the gray gets darker.

"As the days grow longer," my grandmother used to say, "the cold grows stronger." And so it does. Cold gray January days, on and on without end, bleak days, one after another, when juncos seek shelter deep in the old rhododendron outside my kitchen window, huddling among its leaves curled tight as a child's cold fingers inside a mitten, and squirrels stay snuggled in their tree-trunk nests, their tails wrapped around them like winter scarves.

## II

MY HOUSE IS PERCHED on the side of what geologists call the Second Watchung Mountain, though with its five-hundred-foot elevation, it's more a ridge than a mountain. From the front door, you can look far off to the east and, on a winter day, see the skyline of New York City and pick out the tallest buildings, then look southeast across the valley all the way to the ridge of the First Watchung Mountain and, to the left and right, along the horizon, follow the curve of the earth. Most of the year, though, you see trees, the tangle across the road at an edge of the two-thousand-acre Watchung Reservation, which stretches out between the ridges, and the canopy of treetops over the neighborhood below.

From the woods across the road, a deer emerges on this bleak January afternoon etched in shades of gray; like a ghost it materializes from the tangle of trees and wanders up my driveway. Something is wrong. It can't put any weight on its front left leg without it buckling all the way to the ground. The deer hobbles up into the bushes, looking, looking, taking a painful step, then another, always looking. Was it injured by a car, a fall, a mistimed jump? It seems to be seeking shelter in the lee of my house, shelter from the dangers of the woods, from the coming snow. Despite years of deer wars, I feel no hatred toward this enemy straggler, who, without the use of a leg, has lost the very essence of what he is, of what makes him a deer, who has come here, to my yard, seeking refuge. Could I set out some apples? Would he know I was trying to help or would that frighten him? What if he took up camp in my yard, what would I do? If he died here? I think of him as the snow arrives with the dark, another freezing wintry night to get through, to survive, wet, cold, starving, frightened, alone, a night when the cold is an enemy trying to break into the house, and the next morning I'm out early looking for him, searching for his tracks, but the dusting of snow holds no clues of his fate.

## III

IT DOESN'T SEEM TO SNOW ANYMORE the way it once did. Of course, when I was growing up, weather forecasting had none of the computer-model sophistication it has today; a hurricane would slam into a coastal town that wasn't ready for it, and snow would arrive without warning. As a result, children back then seemed to have much more of an influence over the direction and intensity of a storm, so that a school filled with students intent on a snow day could, just as a lightning rod attracts lightning, actually draw a blizzard into town.

Maybe we had some sixth sense about storms. Maybe,

like animals, we could feel a change in atmospheric pressure and sense when a storm was approaching. However we did it, we always seemed to know with uncanny prescience when a big one was on the way. We knew just what sort of day was a blizzard breeder, the necessary weight and texture of the clouds, the exact sickly gray-yellow hue of the sky, the specific temperature that would be best, the precise feel of the air, and when these conditions converged, our teacher would be hard-pressed to keep our attention as we'd sneak glances out the oak-framed windows to make sure the conditions held, passing folded notes to establish the telephone chain if someone learned that school was closing.

To get the kind of accumulation we needed, the snow would have to start in earnest by suppertime, and it had to be the right kind of snow. Several times between supper and bed—repeatedly, actually—my sister and I would turn off all the lights in a room and pull back the curtain to check how it was doing. None of that Robert Frost "easy wind and downy flake" stuff for us; nor were big wet flakes acceptable, or snow that fell tentatively, like it was finishing up for the night. Such snow would be shamed by our hisses and boos. We were looking for a snow with a seriousness of purpose, a heavy, hard, steady snow that wasn't going anyplace anytime soon, and we'd fall into sweet sleep with its steady swish against the storm windows.

Instantly, on waking, we'd know even before we looked. There wouldn't be a sound. Not a car passing by. Not the push and scrape of a snow shovel. Not the grinding rumble of the city's snowplows. Total, absolute, pristine, wonderful silence, which could mean only that the snow was so deep it had shut down the city. Snow Day!

Snow stuck to the storm window, covering it. This was a good sign; there must be just enough moisture in it for perfect snowmen, for snowballs and forts. A dash to a window in the front of the house: outside, a silent snowbound Currier & Ives winter morning. We were expert surveyors then, and by bouncing from window to window, we took all the necessary sitings and triangulations to gauge its depth—eighteen inches, a good two feet at least, two and a half, three feet, as high as the top step out the front door, higher than the wall around the terrace at the back of the house, deep enough to turn the bushes by the porch into mounds, and down the side of the driveway, wind-swirled drifts that could cover a car. Oh, yes, this was a snow day, no questions asked, no debate about it, no worrying that there would be a delayed opening. This was a snow day, and maybe even with a little luck, a two-day cleanup.

As Mole in *The Wind in the Willows* knew, "the best part of a holiday is perhaps not so much to be resting yourself, as to see all the other fellows busy working." A snow day was even better than that; it was an unexpected holiday for everyone, a gift of a pure day. Whatever had been planned had to be canceled, no explanations or apologies required. What errands and chores should have been done couldn't be. We were isolated by the storm, enveloped together in the house, with a fire in the fireplace and a long do-nothing day stretching endlessly ahead: a snow day was more wonderful than a Saturday or Sunday or any holiday.

After breakfast, shoveling out was the first order of business. By the time our mother made sure we were properly outfitted in bulky layers of heavy woolen clothes, shirts and sweaters and stiff winter coats, snow pants with straps that went under the foot, those black galoshes that buckled up the front, cumbersome mittens and itchy ski caps covered over with a hood tied too tight under the chin, attire that would have been excessive for explorers on a three-month expedition across the ice floes of the Arctic, we would have agreed to do anything to get outside. The idea of shoveling seemed an adventure, humanity against the elements, and off we waddled down the stairs to the garage to get the shovels.

Opening the garage door was like raising the curtain on a spectacular stage setting: the storm had taken away our familiar world and replaced it with the Yukon. Either we were a lot shorter then or those snows truly were monumental, for it was all we could do to hopscotch through the virgin depths up the drive to where the sidewalk should be and, shovelful by shovelful, begin to clear a single-width path through the snow into the house.

There were always gangs of older boys (dressed in flannel shirts and jeans, with a ski band around their ears and boots flapping open) who'd come house-to-house to shovel driveways for a few dollars and neaten up our wavering paths where we thought the sidewalk, more or less, should be, so there was plenty of time to get on to the real business of building the forts from which bombardments would be launched and repulsed. If the conditions were just right, you could cut out building blocks from the snow in the backyard and stack them up and smooth them together, igloo-fashion, to construct a pretty formidable fort that would be stocked with rounds of snowballs. Later, when a truce was called, the old wooden toboggan our parents had when they were growing up was hauled out of the furnace room for rides down the hill along the side of the house, all the way to the back of the yard, and once that path was established, the runway was perfect for the sleds and plastic flyers.

By dusk, when our neighbors started drifting home and we had filled the bird feeders with sunflower seed and suet, the buckles of our galoshes were embedded with snow and ice, ice pellets stuck to our mittens and filled our shoes and socks, and every layer of clothing was pretty well soaked with sweat and snow and smelled like wet wool. We sat by the fire-place with mugs of hot chocolate laced with marshmallows as the oak-log embers sputtered and flared colors when our father tossed in a handful of the special salt powder, and we read in the flicker of the flames whether school would be closed again tomorrow.

# IV

THIS WAS REAL SNOW, not today's slushy mess that's gone before the week is up. January snow froze solid and stayed around, day after day getting older, more scarred, pitted, stained, finally overstaying its welcome until it became as tiresome and oppressive, as maddening, as the snows of Willa Cather and O. E. Rölvaag.

Physicians don't talk about it, but it's a fairly simple mat-ter to self-diagnose when you're coming down with snow madness; the symptoms are obvious and easy to spot. Com-plexions assume the waxy tallow sheen of candles. You feel too hot inside the house and too cold outside. Family mem-bers begin casting black looks at you as if, when arguing about the most inconsequential trivialities—which are all that is talked about now—they are contemplating setting your mattress ablaze as you sleep. You begin to feel an uncomfortable physical pressure in being housebound, and when you step outside to escape the pressure, you feel hemmed in by the frozen drifts that loom above the narrow walkways. Every single time you pass the Burton house, you stare at the discolored spot in the snow where a dog relieved itself weeks ago, and by the corner of the Picketts' driveway, you kick that annoying jagged edge of ice again to try to break it off and again hurt your toes and again stomp at it with your heel, and still the accursed chunk won't break off, and the sound of the snow crunching under your feet becomes as grating as Mr. Stoltz dragging his fingernails across the blackboard, and you track in grit and salt. Life has become mere existence. Bundled up, winter-weary, you plod along day after day. "Spring is too far away to comfort even by anticipation," Joseph Wood Krutch wrote of these depressing days, "and winter long ago lost the charm of novelty. This is the very three A.M. of the calendar."

When such symptoms persisted for more than a week or two and you felt yourself teetering close to the abyss of snow madness, a sure antidote was to visit one of the local greenhouses. My favorite was a rather small one attached to a garden center and gift shop where, the snowy January I was in the seventh grade, I went to buy plants and supplies for my science-fair project.

To open that door from the gift shop into the greenhouse

was to walk right into a tropical rain forest, a humid, fragrant jungle so impenetrable that a pith helmet and machete seemed appropriate. Lush, shiny leaves and feathery fronds spilled over every wooden table, poked out from under the benches, crept over the mossy white pebbles of the walkways, pushed up and out at the glass. There were bushes whose branches were laden with miniature oranges, tables of African violets with white, pink, and purple blossoms, benches of strangely shaped, succulent cacti protected by fearsome spikes that made you tingle just looking at them, trays of tiny seedlings and coleus cuttings, palms growing up from giant pods, the sensuous waxy flowers of hibiscus and vining jasmine, ferns hanging from the ceiling, tumbling in luxuriant profusion, coffee plants and ginger plants and snake plants and philodendron with smooth leaves and variegated leaves and jagged indented leaves, geraniums, a Christmas cactus cascading with orchidlike flowers, an enormous rubber tree that must have been decades old, plants with curious fleshy leaves and fuzzy leaves and knobby spiked leaves that had to be touched, a trellis here and there tangled in vines of exotic unknowns. And the heavy moist air held the wonderful fragrance of damp sphagnum moss and potting soil and sand, the citrus of the lemon trees, April's aroma of hyacinth, the green chlorophyll smell of leaves, of growing, of living, of life.

Scurrying in and out of this jungle was a wiry old man who, at his workbench in the corner of the greenhouse covered with a jumble of projects, seemed to me as remarkable as a medieval alchemist. I remember Ted always in a red plaid shirt, a ubiquitous pack of Camels in his shirt pocket. He had, always, a day-old white stubble, dirt packed under his fingernails, and his hands, constantly moving, looked as though they would always be the color of potting soil, even if scrubbed and scrubbed.

Ted was absorbed in his work and would let customers wander around his greenhouse for as long as they wanted without bothering them; but when he learned I was working on a science project about the propagation of plants, those preoccupied eyes behind the thick glasses with heavy black frames became the eyes of a fellow seventh-grader opening up a much-hoped-for chemistry set on Christmas morning.

I had been working that winter on our jalousied side porch, planting seeds saved from the Halloween pumpkin and breakfast grapefruit and oranges, poking toothpicks into an avocado and suspending it in a glass of water, collecting spores from the underside of fern fronds and germinating them in a terrarium, cutting off the tops of carrots and turnips and a slice of a potato and watching them grow into new plants. Ted took me on a crash graduate-level course in botany. He showed me how to unpot a snake plant and

divide it into five plants; how to take a leaf from a rex bego-
nia, cut some slits into the veins of the leaf, fasten it down on
the soil with unbent paper clips, and wait for roots and leaves
to form. He explained what vermiculite and perlite were and
in what proportions they should be mixed with potting soil or
soil from the garden; the differences between clay pots and
plastic pots; how rooting hormones were best applied in
making cuttings; the uses of fertilizers and plant foods. He
knew the Latin names of all the plants in his greenhouse and
used them conversationally until they became as familiar as
my own. He taught me how to take a gratula plant and cut
off a ring of bark on one branch, rub the cut with Rootone,
wrap the cut in sphagnum moss and surround the moss with
plastic held on by rubber bands. A new plant would grow at
the incision. I watched, as I would have watched Dr.
DeBakey perform open-heart surgery, as Ted grafted a section of an oxilo tree cactus (the scion) onto an obruntal cactus (the stock).

That winter our side porch became a plant laboratory,
the wooden shelf along the windows covered pot to pot with
experiments. I dug through the snow and hacked out a
bedraggled pachysandra, brought it into the garage for a day
to thaw, cut the roots into pieces, and planted them to see if
they would grow. Episcia runners were held down in another
pot to root. Geranium cuttings were placed side by side in

water, potting soil and vermiculite to see which grew the best. Endless variations of sun and shade were tested, varying amounts of rooting hormone were applied, measurements of roots and shoots were taken with the precision of an ophthalmologist, experiments were conducted in hydroponics and in growing plants under artificial light.

The creation of this home greenhouse, and the frequent visits to Ted's that the science project necessitated, no doubt staved off any serious seizures of snow madness that long, cold winter.

No longer can you get into your car on a winter's day and be in an Ecuadorian rain forest in ten minutes. Ted's greenhouse and the whole garden center of which it was a part are long gone; a concrete and glass office building and huge parking lot occupy that sunny spot. The veteran's greenhouse on Mountain Avenue where we'd buy fresh-cut carnations was demolished years ago for more suburban homes. And Mary McDonald's greenhouses across from the school are gone now, too. Now flowers and plants are shipped in overnight from places where they're less expensive to grow, and it's almost easier to fly to Ecuador than to find a greenhouse nearby. Today doctors diagnose the melancholy-inducing days of January as seasonal affective disorder and note its symptoms as depression, a craving for carbohydrates, excessive sleeping and social withdrawal, and treat it with light therapy, exposing the patient to strong light to try to trick the brain into thinking it's not really winter. Maybe that works, though walking into the dry cleaner's on a January day of freezing drizzle and sleet, smelling spring and seeing the narcissus in bloom on the counter, can sometimes provide all the fix you need.

## V

LIKE A SWIMMER ON THE STARTING BLOCKS, the world awaits spring, muscles tensed, quivering with anticipation to leap through the air at the crack of the starting gun. With winter not even half over, a crocus on the sunny south bank below the brick walks thinks it hears the signal one day in a February warm spell and opens its yellow flower to the sun. The myrtle nearby sees it and tries out some blue blossoms. Determined daffodils poke up through the heavy wet soil as if the time indeed were now. The goldfish in the brick pool outside the living room windows come to the surface looking for you, expecting once again that their food will be served on a silver platter at high noon, and even a frog has come out of its long sleep from the muck at the bottom of the pool to sit for a while on top of the heater, keeping its bottom warm while it contemplates whether it really is time to wake up.

Gardeners are not immune to such irrational exuberance, to jumping the starting gun, to thinking, against the weight of all experience and evidence and common sense, that maybe this year will be different, that maybe the winter's back has been broken, that the crocus and daffodils, the goldfish and frog and the ever optimistic forsythia, must know what they're doing: spring will be early this year. And so we start making plans.

Spring cleanup first; pick up all the twigs and sticks and branches that have come down in the storms and blustery winter winds. All those acorns on the lawn that the squirrels never got around to, they'll have to be raked up with the bamboo rake. Those weary old oak leaves that eluded the last raking of fall and have been skittering around the terrace all winter and blown into corners and lodged under bushes, get all of those out, too. The big viburnum that hangs over the brick path in back needs to be pruned down a good three or four feet before the leaves break; it's too high already, and with every rain it hangs over the pathway and gets in the way. Now is the time to do it so I don't crush the fern and hosta around it later. (The wispy remnants of a bird nest dangle from the crotch of one of its overhanging branches, just a few inches over my head. As I passed back and forth last spring, did the mother and her babies freeze in terror, hiding up there like the Frank family in the attic annex?) The teak benches and chairs on the terrace should be cleaned with a once-over-lightly Clorox-soaked sponge to remove the moss and dirt without stripping the weathered gray patina. Will have to get the hose out to rinse them off well. From the front beds, last year's annuals have to be yanked out—the first snow came too quickly while they were still blooming, and their bleached skeletons have stayed there since—and the soil in those beds has to be cultivated and maybe some fresh soil from the nursery dug in to bring in some new nutrients; it's worth it, they'll do better this season. Is the nursery open yet? February 4? Better call first. (Maybe better not call. They'll know right away who it is even if I don't tell them, even if I try to disguise my voice: the one they have to scold every spring for insisting on buying a carload of flats of annuals weeks before they sanction their planting. "I'll keep them in a cold frame for a few weeks," I have to promise before they'll let me take them home, as they look at me suspiciously while running my American Express card through the machine. Like they don't believe I really have a cold frame. Which I don't. I start planting the minute I get them home. Some spring soon, I'm afraid they're going to ask for proof, and like a teenager with a fake ID, I'm going to have to procure on the streets a fake cold-frame certification.) While I'm out front, I should really clean out the goldfish pool. This will necessitate putting the goldfish in a clean garbage pail filled with water from the pool and dredging all the debris and gunk so the water will be clearer this year, but that's one heck of a messy all-day job, and maybe that could wait until next weekend. Some of the stones in the wall down by the road were hit by the snowplows and have to be straightened out; that's where the daffodils will be blooming first, so it should look neat and should be done right away. The lavender must be cut back before the new growth starts, and some of the bricks in the paths were shattered by ice, and those should be dug out and replaced with extras from the pile of old bricks behind the oak at the back of the yard, and that hemlock the ice storm bent over, that's got to be cut back or, better yet, braced up. I could drive a metal rod into the ground behind it, out of the way, and tie a green cord from the tree to the rod to hold it up. And there are some of those winter weeds in the beds that should be dug out while they're weak and haven't started sending their roots miles into the soil. Every weed rooted out now will save a lot of work all season.

There's a lot to do. So I get out the trusty old garden cart and haul it up to the back of the yard.

High overhead, a hawk soars like a U2 spy plane, back and forth with just the tilt of its wings, observing everything, nothing escaping its notice. A gentle wind blows in the pines as if to blow away winter, and in the sun it's getting warm enough to take off my sweatshirt and hang it over a dogwood branch. I start picking up winter's debris while contemplating some of the benefits of global warming, feeling quite virtuous to be getting a jump on the season for once. With these chores out of the way, I'll be able to devote the necessary time to planting, rather than rushing it as always happens. As I work, I keep looking over my shoulder as if I've gotten away with something: this was the best that old man winter could dish out? What a wimp!

But the Arctic Express roars through that night, and the next day what was forecast as rain turns into a determined February sleet and then wet, heavy snow that makes tepees of the pine and spruce across the road, and the yellow flower of the crocus shivers in shock and the green of the daffodil shoots turn the dead color of frostbitten fingers with the onset of gangrene, and the goldfish have dived deep out of sight, and the frog is at the bottom of the pool with a blanket of muck pulled over its head as it falls back asleep to resume its wait for the real coming of spring.

The garden cart in the garage, work gloves and pruners resting on it where I left them, waits, too.

## VI

GARDENERS BY NATURE, perhaps, but definitely by necessity, are patient. They plant bulbs on a raw November weekend, knowing that it will be months, the longest months of the year, before they see the results on warm spring days. They have faith that the packets of seeds started inside early in March will become beds of cutting flowers by July. They can visualize how the four-foot-high pines they manhandle home from the nursery and plant along the back border will fill in and grow up, and not next year or the next but years later will form exactly the desired backdrop. They tinker with the garden plan year after year to bring it closer to their concept of perfection, and when something doesn't work out, they make new plans for next year. They plant a sapling that will not in their lifetime mature into the shade tree they know will be just right for that spot, yet they plant it eagerly, expectantly, hopefully, confident that someone else will appreciate its placement. Thomas Jefferson, always the farmer, always the gardener, was well into his final years "still planting trees, to yield their shade and ornament a half a century hence . . . too old to plant trees for my own gratification, I shall do it for my posterity."

Waiting, you learn that everything in time comes to you, that if you are patient enough and wait long enough, you will see it all. There is never any need to plan a safari or adventure of discovery; it's all right here. "I have travelled a good deal in Concord," Thoreau told us. In time, everything in Concord will reveal itself to you, just as Emily Dickinson, who lived her life in the same house in Amherst and "never saw a moor" and "never saw the sea," discovered the entire world was there at her doorstep. Having spent her life as a travel writer "wandering the world," Jan Morris found, as she said, that "the truest truths are small ones, to be discovered wherever you are. If I could have my time over again, I think I would choose to roam only my own small patch of country—my bro, as we say in Wales. Instead of exploring continents and empires, I would investigate ever more intensely our modest fields, hills and villages; rather than wild beasts of Africa, I would watch the herons on the river, the frogs in the pond." For those who wait and watch, it's all happening right outside the window.

Each day is a pageant, a play, produced just for those who are watching, from the drum roll as the watercolor wash of dawn behind the ridge raises the curtain on another day, to the sun's journey westward, the shifting light and shadow, the shaping and reshaping of clouds and their travels across the sky, the endless subtle changes of the day, the infinite variety of days, the coming of night with glimpses of the far reaches of the universe in starlight that, since the days of the crusades, has been traveling through space for us to see at that moment. Each stage setting—be it a rainy day of gloom and fog or a spring day of promise—is a spectacle. The orchestration is a symphony of the wind in the trees and under the eaves, the song of birds, the drone of insects, the squeak of fresh snow, the rustle of fallen leaves. The greatest actors and actresses people this theater of the day, the mailman making his rounds, commuters rushing to work, the landscaper blowing leaves into the road, teenagers walking home from school, everyone playing out the dramas and comedies of their lives that make Shakespeare's and Shaw's seem contrived and simplistic. The show goes on and on yet never repeats itself. Each act you happen to see is a grace, a gift to be opened now, that will not wait until you're ready.

We walk through these most wonderful of stage settings every day, maybe stopping to glimpse a part of the action once or twice, more likely not seeing any of it. "The morning wind forever blows," Thoreau wrote in *Walden*, "the poem of creation is uninterrupted; but few are the ears that hear it." Daily we pass blithely through the halls of museums and galleries more spectacular than the Louvre and the Metropolitan. When for a moment we suddenly see and listen and feel, life is enchantment. Longing to be free of the demands of the presidency, Thomas Jefferson wrote of his "interest or affection in every bud that opens, in every breath that blows." A leaf examined becomes a work of art as if mounted, matted, and framed. How yellow the dandelion, how remarkable its transformation to the powder-puff seed head, how incredible the dispersal of its seed in the wind. What mysteries a rock by the side of the road contains, what stories of explosions of worlds and ice-bound ages it could tell if we knew how to listen. "My profession," Thoreau wrote in his journal on September 7, 1851, "is to be always on the alert to find God in nature, to know his lurking-places, to attend all the oratorios, the operas in nature." Wasn't that other world traveler, Emily Dickinson, on the same search in her poems? "Attentiveness without an object," Simone Weil once said in words that could have been describing Emily's curious poems, "is the supreme form of prayer." Why are we here? John Updike was asked over a century later. "We are here to give praise" was his answer. "I describe things," he added, "not because their muteness mocks our subjectivity but because they seem to be masks for God."

## VII

TODAY THE SUN IS BLINDING on the snow, so bright it seems focused with a mirror, and the snow is melting on the roof, dripping off the gutters, splashing through the drainpipes. It sounds like a faucet has been opened wide, with gallons and gallons of water racing through the leaders, and still there is a cover of snow on the sunny roof, melting. I put my hands around the leader by the front steps and feel the cold water flowing, the ice age breaking up. There are puddles on the steps where drops of water are falling from the roof with the erratic rhythm of a leaky faucet. From underneath the old pile of frozen snow at the top of the driveway where the plow pushed it weeks ago, a rivulet of glacial melt, steady and sure, flows down the driveway to the road, along the side by the rock wall below the barberry hedge, down into the storm drain. The sun is squeezing the ridge like a sponge, and all the excess moisture trapped in the soggy soil by the winter freeze is draining out, running downhill to join the streamlet splashing toward the drain, to join the hollow rush of water somewhere beneath the road, flowing down, always down, washing winter away, down to the river Styx.

"It is about five o'clock in an evening that the first hour of spring strikes," Elizabeth Bowen wrote in *The Death of the Heart;* "autumn arrives in the early morning, but spring at the close of a winter day." A strange observation that holds true again this year. As we shovel and salt the driveway each morning before work and trudge onward with our heads down, watching for black ice, bracing for the next storm, winter has gone away. Maybe the paperboy is ahead of schedule this afternoon, maybe there is something about the way the sun is setting behind the oaks and the way it's on the pine tree in the backyard, maybe it's the smell of air almost too warm for gloves that is of winter breaking up. Whatever, by five o'clock spring is here, and an hour or two later the peepers down in the swamps around Surprise Lake merely confirm what we already feel: the waiting is over. Spring has risen. Spring has risen indeed. May it be so.

❖ ❖ ❖

PLANNING, PATIENCE, persistence: the three human ingredients necessary to create a garden.

Winter is a long time, and exactly what you planted last year and where you planted it become as fuzzy as a squirrel's memory of everywhere it hid stashes of acorns. Jotting notes in a gardening notebook of what is where and what blooms when and other observations will, over the years, facilitate the planning and development of what can become a special garden.

Patience may be a virtue, but virtues may wear thin as winter drags on and the gardener wants to get to work. There's always something that can be done, even in a snowbound winter, from trimming and pruning when you can see the skeletal form of bushes and trees, to wandering around the winter garden and visualizing, from this perspective, what changes might improve it, to reading about other gardens in books and magazines and trying to understand what tricks make them look so good.

Any serious gardener could give courses in persistence. At one time or another, everything will go wrong, and sometimes everything will go wrong at once. Yet the gardener will be back out there every time, looking for all the world like Churchill after Dunkirk, the determined gaze, chin thrust forward, wielding a trowel and clippers, growling in words and tone not subject to misunderstanding: "We shall never surrender."

# Spring Fever

# I

"THERE IS NO DOUBT that Marley was dead," Charles Dickens tells us at the beginning of *A Christmas Carol*. "This must be distinctly understood, or nothing wonderful can come of the story I am going to relate." Understanding all about death, gardeners appreciate, revere, worship spring's wonderful story of life.

How dead is dead? Dickens lets us know just how dead Marley was: he was "as dead as a door-nail," and there was absolutely no doubt about it, for "the register of his burial was signed by the clergyman, the clerk, the undertaker, and the chief mourner." For plants in winter, there are different degrees of dead. The pachysandra, the English ivy, the dianthus, the azaleas, the rhododendron, the butterfly bush certainly look bedraggled and a lot the worse for wear, but the register of the burial has yet to be signed. Keep them on life support and they'll pull through. But most of the others seem as dead as old Marley. The clematis that wound so luxuriantly over the entrance arbor couldn't be more dead, just the skeletal remains, whipped and frayed by winter winds; the ferns, the hosta, the coreopsis, the daisies: these plants that had been pure life have disappeared, departed, gone, it would seem, from this world to their reward.

And then there comes a day.

It's a Saturday morning, a blowy, sunshiny day, a day when the seasons have changed as distinctly as if a calendar page has been turned. Winter sneaks up on us like a thief, its icy fingers picking our pockets, but spring enters our lives triumphant, dancing and singing across center stage.

The big glass door at the dry cleaner's is propped open to let the breeze in, and Marie is practically dancing back and forth behind the counter, welcoming each customer.

"I feel, I feel," she says, giggling, "I feel like, like just getting in the car and taking a drive! Do you know what I mean? Not to go anywhere. Not to have to get somewhere, you know, at a definite time. Just to get in the car and drive, drive just for fun. Yes? Yes! Good morning!" she continues without pause as the next customer walks in and she counts the shirts and, tying the sleeves together, throws them in the hamper and rings up the cash register. "Good morning! It's a beautiful day, yes?"

Yes, it is a beautiful day, and everyone feels it. The attendant in the booth at the parking lot behind the bank who usually stares, suspiciously, as if he expects you to try to floor it out of there without paying the thirty-five cents you owe if you park for more than fifteen minutes, smiles and waves you through: "No charge. Have a good day!" There are lines at the hardware store, customers waiting restlessly at the counter with their dreams and their rakes, shovels, galvanized watering cans, coils of liquid green garden hose, trowels, pruners, a red wheelbarrow without a scratch, bags of fertilizer, boxes of grass seed, oscillating water sprinklers, aerosol cans of weed killer, stakes, twine, brooms, packets of seeds, work gloves: everyone is anxious to do everything at once. Over at the car wash, a man and his golden retriever sit on the curb in the sun, eyes closed, waiting for their car to come through, and a few of the teenage boys drying and polishing the cars have stripped to the waist, their T-shirts hanging from their belts.

As I walk down to Memorial Field that afternoon, I see everyone out working in their yards. Husbands on ladders braced against the sides of their homes are scraping and sanding and painting and cleaning out the gutters and hammering on shingles and taking down storm windows and putting up screens. A couple paces back and forth across their front lawn, looking at one spot as if examining a sculpture in a museum, gesturing, pointing, laying plans for where the azalea will go. Old Mrs. Anderson is on her hands and knees on a mat in her front garden bed, cultivating the soil, tossing rocks and clods into a bushel basket beside her. She looks up and waves and says something that is distorted by her neighbor's leaf blower and the distant whine of a chain saw. I wave back. Two cars roar up Prospect Street and stop next to each other in the middle of the road; teenagers, like tigers from a cage, jump out of every door, shouting and laughing, change cars, slam the doors, and take off.

Save for an occasional jogger around the track, the field has been deserted all winter. Now the tennis courts are full, with gawky beginners and graceful experts; children clamor over the jungle gym and slides and swings and are earnestly at work in the sandbox; young parents push strollers up and down the footpaths in the sun. There's a pickup game of bas-ketball over by the field house—"Here! Over here! Baxter! Baxter! Baxter! Shoot!"—and out in the far field a softball game is cheered by fans on the bleachers and in lawn chairs. How many times may these scenes be repeated and never get old? A dog chases a Frisbee out on the football field, and squirrels chase each other around and around the old sugar maple by the concrete shuffleboard, and sitting on the bench an elderly couple in jackets and berets hold hands, watching, smiling. The same way people always smile at a baby, everyone today is smiling at the warm breeze and the sweet smell of the grass and the way the sunshine lights the fields. Every day from now on won't be like this, we know; there'll be mad March days that we butt through like John Masefield's dirty British coasters, and March nights full of rain and the wind roaring through the trees like surf booming along the coast. But today the glad tidings of rebirth and resurrection have been heard, and that's enough to carry us through.

Back home, Pat and Tony are blowing the leaves out from around the front shrubs. For over twenty years, we've worked together to landscape this shy half acre, so long that we think alike and discuss plans in our own special shorthand. They wave and turn off the leaf blowers, take off their ear protectors, and come over to shake hands. We greet each other like survivors and talk about how hard the winter was and make plans for what has to be done. The official cleanup has begun. The year's at the spring for sure.

Let us pray.

# II

YOU CAN PRAY, of course, anywhere, anytime, whenever you feel like it, but at the beginning of the season, in a ritual sort of like the blessing of the fleet, gardeners flock to the nursery to give thanks. It should never be on a weekend, a Saturday or Sunday when the nursery is jammed with infidels asking why their geranium leaves are turning yellow. Better to choose a weekday afternoon when spring is in the air. You'll know exactly when; it's that day when, since morning, you've been looking out your office window at the white clouds moving across the sky before a good sailing breeze and you have to be out there, too, and the hands of the clock are moving so slowly you're convinced the office manager is manipulating the central control mechanism to retard their progress. Like a prisoner readying his cell for escape, arranging his sheets and blanket and pillow in such a way that it appears he's under the covers sound asleep, set up your office as if you had just stepped out for a moment to go to the restroom, then make a break for it. Walk ever so casually, without jacket or briefcase, toward the fire exit, carefully open the door, making sure it doesn't bang behind you and give you away, go down flight after flight of the metal stairs softly, on your toes, listening for footsteps behind you, for a shout that you've been caught—"Get back here!"—your heart pounding, through the fire door, down the corridor, out the side door, staying close to the cover of evergreens in case they're watching from the windows, count to three and dash out in the open to the parking lot, car key ready, get in, crouch low in the seat, start the engine, and slowly, ever so slowly as not to attract attention, head out to the street, turn left, and inhale: you're free!

You haven't been to the nursery since December, when you went on your lunch hour and Tim and Eileen made the two wreaths specially for you in the greenhouse workshop, but you know all the back roads there as if to home. You approach it slowly to savor the moment. Out along the road are the old weathered boards set on trestles and covered with flats of annuals in bloom—tables of pansies, of orange marigolds and yellow marigolds, flat after flat of blue ageratum and fragrant white alyssum and purple alyssum and alyssum in shades of lavender, the red and pink and white begonias with their waxy green leaves, yellow snapdragons, trailing petunias, tiny impatiens. Is anything more seductive than roadside tables of flats of annuals? That was all the nursery stocked when it opened over forty years ago; since then it has grown into a big business, with acres of annuals and perennials and shrubs and trees and a fleet of trucks and an army of workers for landscaping nearby office parks and estates. But it still feels like a roadside nursery, with the same old wooden trestle tables out here by the road, covered in crazy quilts of spring colors, still tempting every passerby.

I park in my usual spot, get out, and stand there, looking around, dazed, like a pilgrim ready to drop to his knees and give thanks.

Tim sees me before I see him.

"Hi!" he calls over, waving. "How are you? Welcome back!"

"Man, it's good to be back. How have you folks been? Was it a good winter?"

Eileen looks over from where she's hanging a cascading potful of New Guinea impatiens that look as delicious as rainbow sherbet.

"Wow, I thought that was you! Hi! All the familiar faces. The winter? Ugh. Don't even mention that word."

Tim laughs. "It wasn't that bad. Well, at least not quite that bad. A little slow for us."

"It really looks great around here," I say, taking it all in. "You've got a lot of new stuff, even more than last year."

"We try. We've been getting ready since, when would you say, Eileen? February?"

"Yup. Groundhog Day, we were out here freezing our groundhog butts off. We've got some really great perennials coming in a few days. Did your Russian sage work out?"

"Did it ever. It was perfect, just like you said."

"I know, that's one of my top favorites. And that fragrance. Mmm. I think it's so lovely. We should be getting in a bunch in gallon pots, really nice big ones."

"Still too early for annuals?" I ask, knowing exactly what the answer will be but wanting to hear it again, like the soothing age-old words of the doxology.

Eileen looks at Tim. They shrug. Eileen says, "Well, you know what we always recommend, about the last frost date being May fifteenth, so to be safe—"

"May fifteenth?" I ask in horror. "May fifteenth? No way am I waiting until May fifteenth!"

The three of us laugh.

"Okay," Tim says conspiratorially, "you didn't hear this from me, and don't go telling anyone around here, but I've started putting mine in already."

"Ah, now we're talking. Live dangerously."

"Yeah," Eileen says, "and when that one late frost hits, you two can come back here and buy them again. And plant them again."

"That's the spirit!"

"Hey, take a look around," Tim says with a sweep of his hand, "and see what we've done. How do you like that wisteria arbor? Pretty neat? Did you see how we shifted some of the more tender annuals back here under cover, where the shrubs used to be?"

"I'll have to take a look."

"Sure, poke around. Make yourself at home."

"Hey!" Rob calls from outside the garden supply shed, waving and coming over to shake hands. "I didn't think there could be room in your garden for anything else."

"I've only just begun."

"Go for it!"

I start off out by the street, stopping at the tables of pansies, which always remind me of springs long ago when my grandparents took me to a pansy farm to select several of those small wooden boxes to bring home and plant. (Like greenhouses, pansy farms—the one we went to covered several acres—have become office buildings.) My favorites still are the traditional ones, their tops the color of an emperor's auburn robes, their crayon-yellow noses and Oriental eyes and mouths as if painted with watercolors on damp paper and highlighted with India ink for the lashes and whiskers. It's probably impolite to stare, and if you do, the trouble is you find yourself grinning and then laughing out loud at those velvet flower faces that seem to be alternately smiling and frowning, with the group staring right back at you, making faces on purpose.

"Hello, stranger."

I turn and look up and refocus my thoughts, faking a cough to stifle my laughter.

"Maggie! Long time no see. Are you playing hooky, too?"

"Of course. On a day like this? You think there's anyone here who isn't playing hooky? I can't wait to get my hands in dirt, can you?"

"I'm ready!"

"We've got to get caught up one of these days. Give me a call, okay? Lunch?"

"It's a deal."

We return, all of us, to the nursery. We come after the desolation of the long dark night of winter. After its fearsome frozen silence, we come as parishioners entering church on Easter morning, rejoicing in the flowers, yes, and the scents of spring that we inhale greedily like sacred incense, surely that, too, but rejoicing also in the looks of exultation, of revelation, on the faces of the gardeners, the true believers, walking slowly, reverently, between the tables of annuals, along the path through the massed containers of perennials, past the field of boxwood and laurel and azaleas and andromeda and firethorn, worshiping, humming hymns of thankfulness and praise.

## III

"LISTEN," the spring peepers down in the swamps around Surprise Lake trilled that first warm evening, announcing the beginning of the celebration of the season of miracles. "Listen: the time is now."

The unexpected snowdrops beneath the wall by the road, the blue scilla back in the wildflower garden, the reddish tinge in the upper branches of squirrel-gray trees, the yellowing of the willow: "Watch," they whisper, "behold the wonder of life eternal."

Then, up through soggy soil, through the twigs and withered leaves of autumn, colored like Easter eggs, yellow, purple, lavender, white—the crocus.

Daffodils, like young children bursting to show you a trick they've just learned, poke through the mud, waiting a moment when the freeze comes again, shooting up another quarter inch the next day the sun hits the south-facing slope, blooming on the very first day of mild weather.

Through that unforgiving stony, packed dirt along the back of the house, which looks like it wouldn't support the toughest weeds that populate railroad yards, without fertilizer or fuss here they come with tropical vitality, here come the hosta again.

Ferns, like cats, leisurely, luxuriously stretching out in the warm sun, unfold their fiddleheads along the brick paths in the woodland garden, exactly where they were last year.

Tulips know darn well they're good-looking and tease you with their burlesque, each day revealing more of themselves, the swelling bud, the appearance of color, the slow, deliberate, dramatic opening, the proud stance of perfection.

White azaleas. Pink azaleas. The snow-on-the-mountain. Dogwoods. Laurel. Rhododendron. The hosannas of the lilacs, can you hear them shout and sing? The greening of the grass. The leafing of the trees.

How could anyone not see what's happening, how could

anyone miss it? There is nothing subtle or cryptic about it. Who wouldn't be a believer, watching breathlessly in reverential awe, as unfathomable wonders, one after another, reveal themselves to us?

# IV

"SEE, I TOLD YOU," my sister says to our parents as I lead them along the paths of old brick that loop through my woodland gardens, "this proves it. There's something wrong with him."

It's a Robert Browning "all's right with the world" spring morning. The sky: azure blue. The breeze: soft, fragrant with the hyacinths along the path. The lawn: lush and green. The oaks: just beginning to leaf, the blue sky behind the dabs of green like an impressionist painting, the clouds like the ones Daisy wanted to push Gatsby around in. The spring flowers, the dogwoods, the crabapple: overnight all at once in bloom.

In the perennial border, the tulips planted on that bleak November weekend are pure drops of color only a child or genius could have conceived, the reds around the old decaying oak stump blazing like pirates' rubies, the yellows around the viburnum glowing like doubloons from Captain Flint's chest.

The back border is Wordsworth's "host of golden daffodils." The dependable daffodils. Even mice and squirrels, which will eat anything from buzzing cicadas to old newspaper, turn up their noses at the bulbs, and teenage deer seem to find their leaves and flowers as distasteful as broccoli. And so, year after year the dependable daffodils herald spring.

The forsythia I planted around the perimeter of the yard over the course of a dozen or more years, a few spindly bushes dug in every spring, a few more in the fall, those six or seven long, ungainly shoots protruding from a burlap-covered root ball that I watered by hand during the first few hot, dry summers, carrying bucket after bucket to them— now they're a yellow hedge taller than we are, impenetrable, buzzing with honeybees, removing from existence my neighbors' houses and yards.

Clumps of violets, the deep purples and Confederates, are blooming along the edge of the path, with some show-offs bursting up between the bricks, spilling all over them.

Flowing from one border of the garden to the other, one of those gifts of the garden gods, a piece of perfection the gardener has absolutely nothing to do with ("For goodness sakes," the gods seem to say to themselves, "look how hard this poor guy's been slaving away out here, let's at least give him one freebie"): drifts of Virginia bluebells, all in bloom, swaying in the light spring breeze.

It is today, right now, as I lead my tour, the precise

moment that comes to a garden maybe once a season if at all, that hour or two when everything is so improbably pristine and perfect, it's like walking into the pages of a glossy gardening magazine.

Yet I'm not hearing any of the oooohs and aaaahs you would from gardening enthusiasts. Rather, I hear, "See, I told you, this proves it. There's something wrong with him."

"What?" my mother asks.

"All those faces!" my sister exclaims, with a dismissive sweep of her hand encompassing the statues of the four seasons (beautifully aged and moss-covered as if stolen from a hidden Renaissance courtyard, the ones I years ago bought at a Princeton nursery on my way home from a business meeting and sited just so after hours of lugging them around on a dolly, trying position after position), and the concrete head of the north wind hanging on the trunk of the oak tree, surrounded by forsythia, and when you walk out of the gazebo and least expect it, there, climbing up another tree trunk, is a cat gargoyle looking back at you over its shoulder, glaring, its tongue flicking malevolent hisses. And maybe a few others (the four musician statues) here and there (the contemplative gargoyle seated on the long teak bench on the terrace), picked up over the years at antique shops and shows (the stone guard dog by the front door and its mate in the front patio garden; when the dealer told me their snarls reminded him of the way financier Henry Kravitz curled his lip, I had to have them) and now an essential part of the garden. The way the sun hits them at different times of day and in different seasons . . . How they look when they're wet with rain . . . When a dusting of snow covers them . . .

"I don't know what it is about these . . . things, but it's got to be some indication something's wrong with him."

Whence comes an interest in gardens, a love of gardening? What makes a garden person?

It's funny what catches a child's attention. *The Tale of Peter Rabbit* was a favorite of mine, and my grandmother read it to me whenever I visited, but of all the charming illustrations of Beatrix Potter, the ones that intrigued me were not those of the cute little bunnies—Flopsy, Mopsy, Cotton-tail, and Peter—or their adorable jackets, but rather of Mr. McGregor's gardening tools: the dibble he used to plant seedlings, the sieve with which he tried to catch Peter, the watering can, the clay flowerpots turned upside down in the toolshed, the old wooden wheelbarrow. The scenes that I examined again and again with minute attention were not those of the rabbits' home or of the breathless chase but of the garden pool with the goldfish and water lilies and the distant view of Mr. McGregor hoeing onions in his garden.

I remember, too, my grandparents' potting shed, which I no doubt associated with Mr. McGregor's. Walking to it

seemed an expedition, down the steps from the shady terrace, past the stone wall, across the lawn patterned in sunlight and shadow under the towering oaks, way down to the
back corner of the yard. The old shed had once been my
uncle's pigeon coop, the perfect size for a child's clubhouse,
with its wooden door flanked by long, narrow chicken-
wire-meshed glass windows, and when my grandfather
opened the door, there was that delicious smell of cloth bags
of grass seed, of clay flowerpots and bags of potting soil and
fertilizer, and I peered in and stared at all the strange sights,
the big bamboo rake hanging on the back wall with the
shovels and spades and hoes, and the neat stacks of pots
arranged by size on the shelves where pigeons once roosted,
and a wooden shelf arranged with trowels and pruners and a
yellow-handled weeder, and curious tools whose purpose I
didn't know, and in the corner, garden hose coiled on a con-
traption that could be wheeled around the yard, and a fertilizer spreader with its mysteriously fascinating gearshift-like
controls.

My other grandmother was also a gardener and created
two gardens that struck me then, and still do today, as fine
art. She had grown up in the city of Newark, New Jersey, at
the turn of the century, in a small house on a tiny lot just a
few blocks from the bustling downtown business district, as
had my grandfather. High school sweethearts, they married

and, by the time they were in their mid-thirties, had five children. In 1925, with the success of my grandfather's law practice, they bought a lovely old English Tudor home on two acres of rolling tree-shaded grounds in the residential community of Short Hills. There, in those heady days of the late 1920s when anything seemed possible, my grandmother, with a landscape architect and William, her full-time helper, created gardens featured in the October 1934 issue of *House & Garden,* gardens whose lush, dreamlike beauty comes through even in those old black-and-white magazine photographs— the connected series of oblong heart- and diamond-shaped beds bordered by boxwood, the formal circular garden pool overhung with willows at the bottom of the slope of the lawn, the perennial beds laid out along stepping-stone paths whose color range, according to the text, emphasized pinks, lavenders, and soft yellows. Each spring, cars lined up along the road and visitors came to peer through the rhododendrons into this garden wonderland.

It's a garden I saw only as a very young child, but it must have made a vivid impression on me, for even now I return to it every once in a while in my dreams, always walking first down the lawn straight to the garden pool, since that would let me know yes, this is it, this is the right garden, this is my grandparents', it's still here. I remember that halfway down the lawn, nestled in among large rhododendrons, was a circular flagstone floor where once had stood a small garden house overlooking the weeping willows and the garden pool. It was long gone even when I was there as a child, and I never saw a photograph of it, but the idea of it fascinated me, and each time we visited, I stood on the flagstones looking down, asking my father to describe again what the little house had looked like.

Every few years I find myself thinking about those gardens, the way I remember them, and before I know it I am taking a detour to see what they look like now, putting on my turn signal and pulling over to the side of the road to peer through the undergrowth as visitors did long ago. All that remains of the formal gardens are two or three scraggly old boxwood, well over seventy years old now, still marking the corner of a diamond or heart no longer there. It's all been turned into grass now. The last of the willows over the garden pool decayed and fell a few years ago, and the pool itself has been dug up and sodded, though the long wooden garden bench where my grandparents sat on quiet evenings to watch their goldfish perform water ballet is still there, a tribute to the workmanship of yesteryear. The ferns along the bank below the road that were shown in the garden design published in *House & Garden* are still there, too, thriving amid a mass of brambles and tangled growth. These are mine, sort of, I sometimes find myself thinking, and I even consider coming back after dusk with a trowel to liberate some, but before such thoughts progress, I put the car in gear and move on.

Is the possibility of such a garden irretrievably gone, or could the present owners reestablish it? Maybe I'll send them a photocopy of the *House & Garden* article. And maybe someday when I drive by, I'll see the heart- and diamond-shaped boxwood beds and the ferns happy to be amid the trailing roses once again. But gardens are such individual creations that this might be like showing someone a photograph of the *Mona Lisa* and expecting they could re-create da Vinci's masterpiece with oil paints and canvas purchased at the neighborhood art-supply store.

The other garden was in Maine, where in 1938 my grandparents bought at Depression prices a fifty-acre estate with a large white Georgian colonial home set on a promontory above Casco Bay, with a row of ancient oaks in front of the house and a lawn you just had to run barefoot through, down to the rocky shore where you could look out across the bay and islands to the Presidential Range of the White Mountains far in the distance. My grandmother went to work again and created in the lawn on the south side of the house a formal sunken garden.

I have an old black-and-white photograph of her out there on the lawn where the garden would be. It was late autumn. The trees bare. Overcast. A raw fall day. My grandmother in a sweater, my grandfather, the innocent bystander, in his city overcoat, gloves, and hat, a makeshift table covered with sheaves of plans that my grandmother is holding down with one hand while pointing with the other as she maps out her strategy—a clump of phlox here, a bed of daylilies there—the steely, determined look of a general in the eyes of this petite, elegant woman who was an accomplished hostess and looked like she had never in her life so much as let a finger touch the soil. Yet I remember whenever we stayed for a visit—and she was in her seventies and eighties then—every morning when I awoke and looked out the upstairs windows, there she was, kneeling on the green pad in her sunken garden, working before breakfast under those old oaks in the early morning quiet—just the whisper of leaves and the chug of a lobster boat way up the bay in the fog—inch by inch moving around the perimeter of the garden, weeding, deadheading, cultivating the soil, maintaining the incredible state of perfection I recognized then, which shows up in every photograph I have of the garden, and which I've never seen in any garden since.

Gardens, those most fragile and transitory works of art, certainly can't be bequeathed, but aren't they where our own gardens come from? Aren't our gardens assembled fragments of our dreams and daydreams, our memories, images, and visions, remembrances of times past, fantasies, pieces of paradise we try to re-create? A garden house half imagined. A perfect perennial border. An enormous green bottle filled with water and set on the wall of a sunken garden. A sweep of lawn. A violet-bordered path through a woodland garden. A garden pool behind the Wayside Inn in Chatham where fat goldfish glided under water lilies. A vine-covered arbor on Chappaquiddick through which you glimpsed Katama Bay. The door-front perennial gardens of Edgartown. Something we've seen. Something that caught our attention on a garden tour or in a magazine, something learned from watching landscapers at an office park or from visiting an arboretum, bits and pieces of knowledge we pick up here and there.

"Whoever is in charge of your flowers is a genius," I tell the gas-station attendant as he hands me my credit card and receipt. Wooden tubs overflowing with cascades of blossoms line the blacktop right next to the busy street. In more attractive containers, they could be featured in a flower show, they're that spectacular.

"Oh," he beams, looking out at them. "Metropolitan. But it's Miracle-Gro every other day. And water them every other day."

"Every other day?" I ask in amazement. I had always followed the Miracle-Gro instructions of every few weeks, when I remembered, and had the time, and felt like it, with those three conditions converging usually no more than twice a season.

"Yup. Every other day. And water them," he says again, making sure I understood the magic formula. And magic it was, if it could really get flowers like that. Get those plants pumped on steroids. Give them a real buzz. I made a mental note to get out the Miracle-Gro and watering can the next morning, and for a moment considered applying it every other day before I realized on reflection that once a week would be a more realistic goal.

Certainly it would have been fun to talk shop with my gardening grandparents, maybe even to have built on what they learned. Take, for example, something as seemingly simple as weeding. On your own it takes years to discover all the tricks. There is an art to spotting weeds before they do their damage, of learning all their deceits, how the clever ones will grow close to your plants and twist themselves in and learn how to look like them; how some, like poison ivy, are masters of disguise and appear in different parts of the property in different costumes; how weekly weed patrols can never be postponed, at least through early August; how you should vary the direction you walk around the yard on your patrols, and do it at different times of day in different lights; in what areas of the garden preemergent-weed killers can safely be spread in March, and how to use spray weed killers judiciously without harming other plants, and when a stronger spray, a brush killer, is necessary.

It's amazing how long it takes to discover what will grow in a particular spot and what won't, and then what looks well together and what doesn't; how to keep the plants happy; how essential an underground sprinkler system is and how its stations should cover not only the lawn but the perimeter plantings; how some plants like certain types of sprinkler heads and abhor others; how essential it is to keep certain critters out of your yard at all costs and how to spot when they have invaded before it's too late; how to prevent any water feature of the garden from becoming what it wants to be, a brown basin of slime and weed; season after season of trial and error, of great plans laid and gone awry, of crushing defeats and tiny victories and unexpected illuminations. But the joy of gardening is developing and molding a personal vision, a vision of the garden that is and only can be uniquely yours, and then, working with the unpredictable canvas of soil, sunshine, and rain and the brushes of trowels, shovels, rakes, hoes, and pruners and the palette of flowers, shrubs, and trees, trying to get as close to the masterpiece in your mind as your abilities and energy and imagination let you. To have seen my grandparents' gardens and glimpsed them in dreams, and maybe to have inherited some of their gardening genes, that's legacy enough.

# V

A FRIDAY NIGHT IN MAY.

You fall asleep thinking of the garden chores for tomorrow, forecasted to be a perfect ten of a Saturday: planting the far border with white and purple impatiens (mass clumps together, white then purple, or alternate plant by plant, white, purple, white, purple? Or back up the white border with a purple border? Or vice versa?); digging out the three overgrown azaleas in the terrace garden and preparing the soil there for perennials, that's what should have been there always, a small summer perennial garden to enjoy from the dining room and on the terrace (the azaleas you put in long ago to fill up the space: that was cheating); patrolling the woodland gardens to see what has to be trimmed; mounting a search-and-destroy mission against new weeds; and, as your mind meanders back along the brick paths, selecting shady sites to plant the twelve large hosta you bought at the nursery on the way home from work that evening—they looked too good not to buy, though once you unloaded them from the trunk, a dozen did seem like an awful lot, about ten more than you really had room for—you fall sound asleep.

You awaken rested, your eyes open wide, your thoughts clear, not a trace of weariness in any joint, sinew, or muscle; in fact, you've never felt better. You're ready to jump out of bed and get started. You turn to look at the clock to see why the radio hasn't come on. That's why: it's only two-fifty-three A.M. Three o'clock in the morning and you're wide awake and ready to go. You think about it—you could start now and get a jump on the day—and only convince yourself that it's way too early by the accumulation of irrefutable evidence: (a) it's not light yet; (b) the grass will still be soaking wet; (c) the neighbors won't appreciate any noise; and (d) whoever might see you out there will likely have the commitment papers drawn and served by eight-thirty A.M., latest. Okay, just have to sleep three more hours.

Again you start visualizing where each hosta could be squeezed in along the paths, which must again do the trick, since next you hear that clear, unmistakable call of the cardinal, the early riser, and know the moment is nigh, and the flicker is tapping out the morning news on the dead oak branch, and then, from the dogwood outside the bedroom window, you hear the morning song of your favorite catbird, the one that comes to eat raisins from your hand, and you know he's looking for you already. You turn and look at the clock radio: close enough. Your feet are on the ground and you're off.

How is it that the prospect of a day spent digging holes in dirt and tucking in plants and watering and weeding and trimming, raking and training, fertilizing and deadheading, spading a bale of peat moss and bags of perlite and vermiculite into the soil, turning it over and over again, can so energize us, when on any given winter's weekday it is all but necessary to hire a crane operator to bring a rig into our bedroom and hoist us out of bed and into an upright position and a front-end loader to push us out toward the door to work?

No doubt what causes gardeners to fall asleep dreaming of weeds and dirt has something to do with those same inexplicable forces that pull golfers out to the links to smack away at that little white ball and that impel fishermen to pull on hip boots and wade out into a river to cast and cast and cast again; these activities constitute socially acceptable reasons for being outside grooving, without appearing to be either an anchorite or a simpleton.

It's that, surely, but something more, too, for how is squeezing out impatiens from a flat and creating a border display with them any different from dabbing drops of oil paint onto a canvas? How is planting them in the spots you think are just right any different from arranging single words on a piece of paper to replicate a vision you imagine? How is sculpting a viburnum distinguishable from chiseling a block of marble? How is laying out a garden design any different from drawing up a set of architectural plans? There is in the gardener something of the artist, and in the irrepressible zeal to garden is the artist's zeal to create.

The prospect of a sunny morning spent bending over, ripping from the earth those particular plants you don't think should be where they obviously want to be, how is it that this can be so soothing, so satisfying, so fulfilling? Maybe you're pretty dense after all. Maybe this is what your calling really is—some sort of repetitive, menial, mindless, meaningless work.

When such thoughts bounce across the brain, it's comforting to remember how Henry Thoreau would hoe his bean fields around Walden "from five o'clock in the morning till noon." And to remember America's Renaissance man, Thomas Jefferson, who late in his life contemplated what he would have been if he could have followed any path: "I have often thought that if heaven had given me choice of my position and calling, it should have been on a rich spot of earth, well watered, and near a good market for the productions of the garden. No occupation is so delightful to me as the culture of the earth, and no culture comparable to that of the garden. Such a variety of subjects, some one always coming to perfection, the failure of one thing repaired by the success of another, and instead of one harvest a continued one through the year." It's comforting, too, to come across what Robert Louis Stevenson had to say about weeding—he, that gifted, prolific author, working in a frenzy to glean his teeming brain, racing the early death he knew was inevitable and fast approaching. From Vailima, his new home on Samoa, he wrote a friend in November 1890 that he had gone "crazy over outdoor work, and had at last to confine myself to the house, or literature must have gone by the board." It seems he was spending every waking minute gardening. *"Nothing,"* he wrote, underlining the word for emphasis, *"nothing* is so interesting as weeding, clearing and path-making; the oversight of labourers becomes a disease; it is quite an effort not to drop in to the farmer; and it does make you feel so well. To come down covered with mud and drenched with sweat and rain after some hours in the bush, change, rub down, and take a chair in the verandah, is to taste a quiet conscience. And the strange thing that I mark is this: If I go out and make six-pence, bossing my labourers and plying the cutlass or the spade, idiot conscience applauds me; if I sit in the house and make twenty pounds, idiot conscience wails over my neglect and the day wasted." The day wasted. Obviously Stevenson felt it, too. A day spent at work—which, in his case, was pretty exalted work—was a day wasted when compared to a day weeding and gardening. It was fulfillment, satisfaction, for Stevenson and Jefferson and Thoreau, a day of achievement, a day spent celebrating life. Is there not in that sense of achievement, in that celebration, something of the same satisfaction the artist feels?

## VI

DIGGING A HOLE large enough for a hosta in a gallon container, let alone a shrub or tree, is no easy matter in my gardens on the side of the ridge. Sometimes you can dig out the first trowelful of soil, perhaps even the first shovelful, but more likely than not, the metal blade sinking sweetly into loam as if into layer cake strikes a rock, jarring wrist and elbow. Then it's time to take the prospector's pick from the garden cart, prying around the edges of the hidden rock with the tip of the pick, feeling its shape, gauging its size, loosening the soil around it, prying it until it wiggles like a loose tooth, then levering it out of the hole or, if the rock won't budge, going to work with a crowbar. Rock after rock is extracted. The hole deepens and widens as bits and pieces of the ancient basalt that form the ridge are cast aside.

What tales a hole dug in a garden could tell, what treasures we unearth, if only we knew how to look. Here are rocks that could speak to us of the earth's violent beginnings, of fiery cataclysmic days when the earth split open, of volcanic eruptions and 200-million-year-old lava flows, of ancient seas, of dinosaurs that walked the mud flats between the Watchung ridges, of the millions and millions of years during which the red shale and sandstone eroded and plants and trees grew and died and decayed and mixed with the shale and sandstone to form the layer of soil over the basalt, of the glaciers that ten thousand years ago advanced twice across the valley. What dirt-encrusted artifacts are cast out of our garden holes as we dig: fern fossils and fragments of dinosaur footprints and dinosaur eggs, arrowheads and broken shells of the Lenni Lenape Indians who camped in the valley and gave the ridges their name, Wach Unks—high hills—traces of the precious copper the early Dutch explorers searched for in the ridges, Revolutionary War musket balls and buttons: all have been found within a half mile of here.

I watch two squirrels chase each other in a hormonal rush, back and forth across the lawn (exactly when did the grass turn so green?), playing hide-and-seek and hard to get, chittering, chattering, using the arbor and gazebo as a jungle gym, scampering all the way up the tall oak, making improbable leaps from branch to branch like daredevil aerialists. (Once a squirrel miscalculated a high-wire leap, fell, and hit the ground with a thud. That's a goner, I thought, but in a moment or two the squirrel got up and crept away to wait for the stars to stop spinning. You see something like that only once.) Just what is it that birds and animals do all day? Foraging for food and water, sure; mating, rearing young, staying warm or cool, watching for danger; but this doesn't take all day long. They must have some time off when they are just messing around. What occupies their leisure moments? Or are they just dozing? Are certain days different from others? Do they have the equivalent of a Saturday? Do they have a routine? Are there rainy- and stormy-day activities? That fissure down the trunk of the oak, it's starting to heal: a lightning bolt slammed into the tree two summers ago and blew out the underground sprinkler system and must have electrocuted the squirrel I found the next morning at the base of the tree. Some of these oaks must be two hundred years old. When my grandfather was growing up a block or two down the road, some of these same oaks were here. They were full-grown then, and that was almost a hundred years ago. They provide so much shade that they, like the rocky soil, limit what will grow here. Maybe these are English conditions; the English boxwood thrives. That wonderful scent of boxwood in the sun, "the flavor of eternity," as the poet Oliver Wendell Holmes described it, reminds me of the old formal colonial gardens of Williamsburg and Monticello, of Mount Vernon, where I bought some of my first cuttings, descendants of Washington's "great billowy masses" of boxwood, and I begin thinking of Washington and Jefferson gardening, hacking their gardens out of the original American wilderness, and remember my first months here after I bought the house, the weeds knee-high throughout the property, pulling out one bushel basketful after another, yanking down endless vines of honeysuckle and ivy and wild grape that twisted and trailed for miles, overwhelmed by what lay between the yard I flailed away in and the garden in my mind.

Here's an oyster shell. I find a few each year, usually after the rain has washed the dirt off. What are they doing here? Could the sea ever have been way up here? Or are they from an Indian campground? Or from a dinner feast held at the turn-of-the-century colonial-revival mansion whose land once included my yard? Nearby, a blue jay takes wisps of dried crocus leaves to weave as a wonderfully soft lining for a nest. Is its nest in the holly? That's where it keeps flying. The holly looks healthy, as always, its leaves bright green; it's over twenty, thirty feet tall now. It must like it here, too. The holly and the ivy. There was a superstition in medieval England that an unmarried woman should tie a sprig of holly to her bedpost so she wouldn't become a witch. We don't really believe in witches anymore, or do we? What kind of people were considered witches? Dragons. Unicorns. From my pile of dirt beside the hole, a cicada stumbles out maybe a few days or a few years too early. Aren't they as bizarre as unicorns? They look fierce as dragons, with those glinty red eyes, but they mean well, these creatures that live underground for seventeen years, waiting for that one special year when they will emerge, sometimes scores of them to the square foot, to climb up bushes and trees and begin their mating chorus that lasts all summer. So what's been happening underground these last ten years, Mr. Cicada? Any good gossip? As I struggle with prying loose and pulling out the next rock, I remember like a mantra Pat and Tony's words about the upside of gardening on a ridge of rock, that the shrubs and trees, once established, will do especially well, their roots working their way deep around the rocks. That's how the weeds take hold. We treat weeds as the enemy. We rip them from the ground. We nuke them with weed killers. We try to annihilate them. But then you think, why are they the enemy, these weeds that cling so valiantly to life, maybe sensing they aren't wanted, whose ancestors have been purged and pulled time and again as they've tried to colonize this land they know, genetically, is meant for them. You have to admire their bravery, their tenacity, their willingness to adapt to whatever they face, compared with your pampered perennials, which wilt and faint if you even look at them the wrong way, let alone do something not exactly to their liking. (Who would know on their own that clematis likes its feet in the shade and its head in the sun, that yarrow likes its soil dry, and coreopsis, a natural to plant near yarrow, likes its soil moist?) From prehistoric man to the Romans to the Indians to the early settlers, some of these weeds have been gathered from the wild and even cultivated for boiled greens and salads. And some of them aren't even bad-looking, in fact they would be interesting specimens if there were just a handful of them in the garden—blue chicory, goldenrod, Queen Anne's lace (even the names are beautiful)—but ye gods are they prolific! (That's why another name for Queen Anne's lace is devil's plague.) How would a bed of dandelions be any different from a bed of marigolds? But for all that loose seed, wouldn't it look every bit as good and be easier to grow? What is my barberry hedge down by the road (with its haze of greenery in spring and scarlet berries in fall) but a cultivated weed that farmers for centuries have eradicated? Isn't every perennial somebody's weed?

On spring mornings when you go outside at dawn to work in the garden—like Thoreau, "rapt in reverie," who "silently smiled at my incessant good fortune"—the next time you think to check, it's afternoon.

## VII

THERE'S THE STORY of the old man who was walking through the woods and came upon a frog sitting along the side of the path near the swamp. "Kiss me and I'll turn into a ravishing young woman," the frog croaked. The old man stooped over, picked up the frog, and stuffed it into his pocket. A mile or so down the path, squished, hot, and cranky, the frog croaked, "Didn't you hear me, you batty old man? I said, kiss me and I'll turn into a gorgeous young woman!" "Oh, I heard you," the old man replied, "but at my age, I'd rather have a talking frog."

Who wouldn't? Frogs are fun.

My frogs have it all figured out. They keep very particular office hours. They don't get up early; none of this early-bird-gets-the-worm nonsense for them. The goldfish are looking for breakfast before seven o'clock, but the frogs don't arise until they feel like it, waiting until the fish have eaten, show-ered, and shaved. Then, around ten o'clock, if—and this is an important if—the sun is out and the day is warm and to their liking, they'll pop up in the pool, their eyes bugging out in either amazement or amusement, board the wooden rafts I built for them, and drift around the pool to see what's been happening and take some sun.

Occasionally one will jump from the raft to the side of the pool, the thrust from his back legs spinning the raft out into the pool, to the momentary annoyance of his fellow rafters. That is just about the extent of their daily activities. Like sun worshipers at a resort, they'll spend the better part of the day just lounging around poolside until you'd think that their reptilian skin, never protected with sunblock, would peel off. They must sense that this is a frog-friendly home or maybe even a frog Easter Island. A frog will hop onto one of the three concrete frogs that sit around the edge of the pool, or onto the bronze fountain frog lying on its back on the bronze lily leaf in the middle of the pool, its hands folded over its stomach, spitting a steady stream of water into the pool, and there take up headquarters, cooling off every now and then by jumping in and doing a leisurely breaststroke across the pool. Thus their entire day is spent, sunbathing and dozing: the epitome of relaxation. By four o'clock, the day's activities (such as they are) being completed, it's down to the bottom of the pool and to bed.

Through eons of evolutionary experience, frogs have learned that they look irresistibly squeezable, and so, like children wary of maiden aunts coming toward them with lipstick-smeared smiles and open arms and wet juicy kisses, they've learned how best to sidestep such encounters. As soon as a frog sees a human form approaching, it emits something between a grunt and a shriek—which startles both of us—and instantly jumps straight into the pool like a youngster yelling "Geronimo!" What frogs lack in swimming ability—they swim like little old ladies with inner tubes stuck around their waists, clutching the edge of the pool with their webbed hands as soon as they reach it, as if they couldn't possibly take another stroke—they more than make up for in their jumping prowess. I've seen them jump six feet from a dozing rest easily, no sweat, gauging their jump so precisely that they land exactly where they want. The pool is three feet in diameter and the bronze fountain occupies a good ten inches in the center, yet the frogs, with no apparent forethought before they take off, so instantaneous is their launch, splash into the water, never crash-landing into the fountain or the edge of the pool. In a few moments two eyes peer out from the now placid water to see what my business there may entail.

A superior intelligence is not a characteristic usually associated with amphibians, yet these frogs have it all figured out: no gainful employment; no stress; a life of leisure—it sure looks like they're doing something right. My first frog even made his way to the pool on his own. Exactly how he did this is a mystery as baffling as how ancient man made his appearance in various far-flung outposts of the world, especially since the nearest swampy area is a good mile away, downhill around Surprise Lake. Could he somehow have sensed a new frog haven, packed his bags, and begun the long uphill trek through woods, across the street, up the side of the ridge, across the road, and up into my front yard?

The pool's other residents, the goldfish, would like to give the impression of being as genteel and gentle as painted koi on ancient Chinese porcelain. In truth, they at times get bored swimming laps and trying out more creative and constant couplings than seen on the afternoon soaps, and seize any opportunity to amuse themselves. The frogs are their chief source of amusement.

On a serene spring morning, as the frogs drift on their rafts and contemplate how all is right with the world, a goldfish will swim up from below and shatter this peaceful scene by ramming the raft until it wobbles back and forth. The frogs try hard to ignore this but look not unlike the victim in Winslow Homer's oil *The Gulf Stream*, clinging to a derelict vessel as the choppy waters explode with pretty evil-looking sharks. If a frog is in the water relaxing, doing the dead man's float, arms and legs stretched out and face in the water, a goldfish will not be able to resist goosing it. If a frog hangs on to the side of a raft with its hands, as if about to strong-arm itself up onto a float, a goldfish will just have to swim between its legs dangling in the water. Like bullies doing cannonballs into a crowded pool, splashing water and making a general nuisance of themselves, the goldfish seem to find their antics endlessly entertaining, even after the frogs make clear that it's all getting rather old.

Perhaps like the indulgent mother who can't see that her darling son is the class bully, I'm quite proud of the intelligence of my goldfish. When the bored teenage salesclerk at the pet shop scooped out a dozen squirming fish and dumped them into the plastic bag of water with one strand of algae shimmering in it, I had no expectations that these tiny quivers of orange that cost a dime apiece would be able to do anything but look pretty in the garden pool. Their new home was ready for them—a veritable Taj Mahal for these humble creatures, a circular pool three feet across and three feet deep, set in the boxwood-bordered brick patio below the windows at the front of the house, a pool Narcissus would have knelt beside to admire the loveliest of them all.

Fish gotta swim, and that's all I was expecting them to do, yet since the April morning I let their plastic bag float in the water for a half hour so that they could get acclimated to their new home, then opened it up and poured them in, they have been overachieving. All on their own. With no elders to teach them or show them the ropes.

Right away they learned which side their bread was buttered on and knew exactly who I was, going into a feeding frenzy whenever I walked over to the pool, lurching up to the surface, staring right at me, their mouths snapping open and shut in a strikingly good imitation of the original *Jaws*. There is no way you'd put an appendage into that pool had they teeth; you wouldn't even want them to gum you. Now, it's not as if they just recognize me as a big something that serves their meals. Many is the time I've watched from the window the neighbor's cat sit at the very edge of the pool, staring and staring in, salivating, drool dripping into the water, and the goldfish, like submarines, run silent, run deep. So there is no way in their unblinking eyes that a cat can impersonate a human, no matter how hard it tries, or that I resemble a cat. But the fish are even more insightful. When I want to show them off to my friends and walk them over to the pool, the goldfish again are in hiding, down deep in the green depths. More than one of me at a time is simply not acceptable. They will do their feeding dance for me any time of day, morning, noon, or evening, even if they've just eaten a half hour before. Yet if I try to lure them up to the surface by sprinkling in a bit of food so that I can show my visitors just how vicious they truly are, maybe one or two will swim up to take a halfhearted nibble and then quickly disappear. What's also interesting is how they recognize me whatever I'm wearing—they've seen me in fall coat and raincoat, workshirt and sweatshirt and T-shirt, Timberland boots, Topsiders—it makes no difference; there's no fooling them.

The intelligence of goldfish shouldn't surprise us. Each spring, all up and down the eastern seaboard, small herring-like fish, alewives, come in from the far surges of the sea, into bays and tidal estuaries, thousands at a time moving up brooks and streams, inland, to the exact freshwater pond where they grew up three or four years before. They spawn and lay their eggs and then return to the sea, their children following them a year later. How is this possible, how can they do that, how can they find their way from the ocean into the very pond of their childhood? And why would they want to? A pond is a pond is a pond. Why, for an alewife, isn't one freshwater pond as good as the next? For some reason it isn't, and they'll beat their brains out to try to return home, flinging themselves again and again at any dam or obstacle as they move up the brooks from the sea.

Some frogs, too, seek home, in the spring return to the location of the vernal pools where they were born. If that particular pool happens to have become part of a parking lot or office complex while they were gone, they'll hop about in a daze, trying to locate the old homestead and figure out what happened to it and what to do.

Migratory birds and butterflies travel thousands of miles, and like Ulysses, much have they seen and known, but these cosmopolitans who could live anywhere, choose, also like Ulysses—no matter how long or hard the journey—to return to the spot where they started, to home. A newt, we're told, can by scent find its way home from miles away. The homing instinct. Is this why my house is within a good stone's throw of where my great-grandparents and grandparents and parents lived? What is it about this sense of home that must be so deeply inbred in all creatures great and small, in eels and in us? Is gardening all about the meaning of place, the nature of time, the happiness of home?

## VIII

SPRING IS LIKE A FIREWORKS DISPLAY: the first rat-a-tat-tat of crocus and forsythia that catches our attention; the sky-rockets and bursts of pure colors of daffodils and hyacinths and tulips; the gasps as the showy lilacs and azaleas open; the boom-boom-boom of the rhododendron and laurel and peonies. And then, sometime in June, the colorful noise stops. The headlong rush of spring to get gardens dug and lawns seeded and trees planted is over. A peaceful green quiet descends like a benediction.

June has that momentary adolescent look of youth, a freshness before everything is chewed and scarred and begins, barely perceptibly, to toughen and yellow and wither. Closing doors is what I always think about on a June day like this. A day when you can almost taste long, lovely kisses in the air. The sort of day that always reminds me of our last days in high school.

June was full of such days then. I remember those leafy green mornings, sitting in darkened classrooms with the overhead lights turned off to keep the rooms cooler, the doors along the hall open for cross-ventilation, and the venetian blinds, drawn against the sun, billowing slowly in a hot breeze and then slapping back against the open windows. I remember the drone of a lawn mower moving back and forth across the far playing fields and the green smell of June grass and the girls in summer-print shifts and leather sandals. And I remember Joanna and Haven, the things we said and what happened that year.

It's something about those late June days. I'll be driving along some street, and the way the branches of the oaks arch over the road and intertwine will remind me of Druid Hill Road, where Joanna lived. Or I'll be daydreaming and start to hear in the leaves moving with the breeze the rhythm of Haven's voice, the rise and fall, his intonations, and then, quite distinctly, fragments of conversations, and pretty soon the three of us will be talking about the things we talked about as we drove under the twining oaks, past the green lawns and houses set back from the street, into those honey-suckle mornings.

They were days of long last looks, of looking at the peo-ple you had been with most of your life, really looking at them, with the sudden realization that you might not see them for ten years or twenty or maybe ever again. You looked at them as if you had never seen them before. Which you hadn't. The nerds. The greasers. The geeks. The hunks. The preppies. The hippies. The clods. The cretins. The stu-dents. The studs. The introverts. The extroverts. The surfers. The jocks. The spazzes. The fat boys. The punks. The friends. The enemies. The perky cheerleaders. The sultry debs. The pot heads and acid heads. The faceless ones whose names you never knew, whom you had never spoken to, or heard speaking, each one, you now realized, someone special you wish you had known. The cutups. The wise guys. The leaders and losers. What would become of them? Suddenly you saw them, the uniqueness of each, and loved them all. One period after another, the classes ended, the students changed rooms and walked down the halls, walked down halls airy with those sweet June breezes, into the crowds, and were gone forever.

There is no place as peaceful as a school a few days after graduation, as hushed as a Civil War battlefield, the parking lot empty, the windows shut, the venetian blinds all pulled to the same level. Walking around the outside of the building and down to the playing fields, you feel like a veteran trying to recall just what the sides had been and why.

Under the trees, shadows drift on the grass and summer insects drone overhead, and as you sit in the shade, you know that although they all are gone, everything here will always be the same. On those blue-sky afternoons of late September, Coach will be out on the field barking orders to the football team. All year long, after school, students will be putting together the newspaper, the yearbook, rehearsing the play; the band will be practicing; Miss Johnson will be tutoring her students in the chemistry lab. And each June there will be several students who spend their study halls outside, in the sun, in love, who do not want it to end.

Mornings, green mornings when time stopped at Thoreau's "meeting of two eternities, the past and future, which is precisely the present moment," driving to school on those leafy green mornings when the branches of the trees arched over the streets and we rode on waves of music and June's dappled light.

❀   ❀   ❀

WHAT YOU WOULD LIKE TO GROW in your garden probably bears little relationship to what your garden would like to
grow. Listen to what your garden is trying to tell you, recognize what makes it unique, and work with its strengths rather
than trying to impose your fantasy vision on it.

Getting plants to grow is just the first step in creating a garden. Through experience, the gardener learns which plants re-
quire the same conditions and grow well together, which
complement one another in size, shape, texture, and color,
which will look well from inside the house and from different
parts of the yard, which can extend the season of the garden.
Getting just the right mixture by trial and error can be as difficult as trying to open a lock without knowing the combination.

A gardener can gain the necessary experience to create a
special garden only through seasons of experimentation, and
the more hands-on experience he has, the more he will learn:
observing the quirks and peculiarities of one's own garden,
going on garden tours, reading gardening catalogs and books
about gardens, talking to other gardeners to get new ideas.

Don't lose sight of the purpose of your garden. Take
some time to sit in the gazebo, to walk around the garden
with no purpose other than to fill your senses, to restore your
soul. June is meant to be enjoyed. "Then, if ever, come perfect days." Lay down the shovel to savor those days.

# Summer Afternoon

# I

"Summer afternoon," mused Henry James, "summer afternoon; to me those have always been the two most beautiful words in the English language."

Nathaniel Hawthorne in Concord knew that "for a few summer weeks it is good to live as if this world were heaven."

And a garden on a summer afternoon, if seen at just the right moment from just the right perspective, can be a part of that fleeting heaven.

By the start of this summer, all the touches of oil paint that for twenty years I dabbed here and there on the canvas of my yard seemed at last to have converged to create a garden that held me spellbound. So few gardening efforts succeed (the plants and shrubs that didn't work out would stock a small nursery) that it's all right to show off the ones that do. Come take a look.

The small English-boxwood-bordered beds set in the brick patio along the sunny front of the house are bursting with primary colors, lemon-drop marigolds in the square beds on either side of the circular goldfish pool with its splashing frog fountain, and farther along the narrow patio, two identical square beds, defined by boxwood, filled with white begonias flanking a circular boxwood-bordered bed the same size as the goldfish pool, planted with blue ageratum. (The plan for this garden emerged full-blown during a tedious office meeting as I sketched it out on the back of an agenda outline and kept track of how many times the word "flexibility" was used.) A row of large American boxwood runs along the foundation of the house and forms the backdrop for this garden. In the middle, set close to the house, is a small clump of birch. Another is at the end of the patio by the front steps (both of which I treat as bonsai and periodically trim to keep them from getting too large), and an old kousa dogwood shades the far end, under whose branches sits a rather fierce stone guard dog, watching. In front of the patio: a swath of lawn with a stone wall below it that begins the terraced pachysandra and laurel drop to the driveway, down the side of the ridge. Walking up the front steps; standing by the door; strolling along the lawn; looking out the floor-to-ceiling windows of the living room: from all angles, it worked. (I know; I've tried all the views, again and again.)

Simple? Yes. Clean, elegant, flowering from April through November (nothing can beat the basic annuals at this). Best of all, how hard would that be to maintain in peak condition all season long?

That's where our garden tour starts, out front. Note how well the flowering crab apple that replaced the dead dogwood below the front steps has filled out; in early May you walk up the steps into its fragrant cloud of white blossoms. Now take a quick look at the postage-stamp-size garden on the driveway side of the steps. In that right angle, water trickles down mossy rocks into a tiny woodland pool surrounded by painted Japanese fern set among small river stones. A meditative Buddha sits contemplating. The white concrete walls of the corner are covered by firethorn (picture the red-orange berries of the firethorn in the fall), and a birch provides a serene canopy.

Over there, halfway down to the road, is a narrow garden bed cut out of the side of the ridge, held up with a small stone wall, filled with red and white impatiens backed up by a border of box. Garden addicts habitually do as much as possible with whatever space they have (and, when there's no space left, are apt to devise plans for how their neighbors' property should be improved and sometimes even contemplate carrying out those plans in stages in the early morning hours).

Next to the center of the garage, in full sun, a planter overflows with a confectioner's swirl of red, pink, and white begonias, tiered like a cupcake. Open the moon gate set in the arbor, covered so completely with clematis that walking through feels like entering a secret world. There begins the brick pathway that leads up the side of the house, past the dark green border of Norway spruce and tall cherry laurel, a few planted each spring, a few more each fall, into the backyard and gardens. The dusky red of the brick pathway (made of used bricks, slightly irregular, mellow with age) is a warm contrast to the coolness of everything green. In shady areas, the paths are inclined to get slippery with moss and algae, which makes walking treacherous. After a year of trial and error, I found a letter in a gardening magazine that provided the solution: sprinkle on Clorox with a plastic watering can a couple of times a season. Don't try to dilute it, that won't do the job. Sprinkle it on straight. And do it on a sunny day; that helps. By the end of the day, the bricks are clean again. An important note to add from experience: buy the ten one-and-a-half-gallon super-economy-size jugs of Clorox when the supermarket isn't crowded; fewer people to look at you as if you have a serious home-cleaning problem or are gathering the ingredients for something illegal.

In years past, as I showed friends around, I felt as if they were seeing only the dabs of paint of some abstract work of art they didn't quite understand, while I was seeing a finished composition that may have been more in my mind's eye than before us. Time is as essential in gardening as rain, soil, and sun. It takes time for the new gazebo to weather and merge from raw wood into the branches around it; time for the teak bench to turn silver-gray; time for the statuary, once stark on pedestals, to make itself at home, to become a little mossy, lichen-encrusted, to have plants cozy up alongside and the lilac and forsythia nestle around; time for the boxwood to fill in and become Williamsburg borders; time for the hedges to grow together and create the walls of a garden room; time for the firethorn to take hold, to decide it likes it here and will stay, covering itself with white flowers in spring and berries in fall; time for the plants to get to know one another and move closer together, to seed themselves and bring new generations; time for the few flying strands of clematis carefully trained up the side of the arbor to stretch over it in a heavy mass; time for violets to sneak in between the brick borders and the myrtle to trail over the sides of the stone steps. And in time, gardens come up with some of the best creations on their own. You may position plants just where you think they should be, but like a woman adjusting her skirt, they all move and shift to find the most comfortable spots. Now, over the years, time had done its work to connect the dots, to complete the painting.

In many ways, gardens, like paintings, are illusions, and

through years of experimenting, gardeners learn some of the illusionist's tricks. As we walk beyond the house and turn, before you is an instant perennial garden, a garden that looks like it's been there forever but was in fact created from scratch last month.

Extending out from the sunroom at the back of the house is the bluestone terrace (each stone separated by army-green moss that took up residence there on its own, thick and luxurious, longing to be stroked), bounded by a curved brick wall that holds the raised perennial bed, backed by a stone wall topped with a boxwood border, beyond which the lawn climbs slowly to the top of the ridge. When I dug out the three old overgrown azaleas in May, all that was left of this garden were some really good bones. The stone wall was an ideal backdrop. In the far corner, shaded by birch and overhanging azaleas, a small waterfall splashes down the stone wall into a garden pool. Dianthus from a mail-order catalog (shriveled stems with a few pathetic root hairs when they arrived years ago) have happily rambled all along the front of the garden, spilling down over the brick wall; the carnation-scented flowers of May and June, and then the soft gray-green foliage, create a season-long front border. There were a few thriving Stella de Oro daylilies here and there, and some ferns against the stone wall. And that was it.

I had tried everything in this showcase garden bed whose

conditions were just about perfect. The soil was well prepared, the garden well protected, it got good sun. What more
could plants want? Apparently a lot more, for each year's efforts petered out in failure by midsummer: my favorite annuals; boxes and boxes of perennials I ordered and planted
following the elaborate plans I devised; creative combinations
of annuals and perennials; those roseform begonias billed to
give marvelous masses of nonstop color. Forget about it,
nothing worked. Every dream crashed into reality. "For my
own part, I am trying to make a grey, green and white garden," Vita Sackville-West once wrote. "This is an experiment
which I ardently hope may be successful, though I doubt it.
One's best ideas seldom play up in practice to one's expectations, especially in gardening, where everything looks so well
on paper and in the catalogues, but fails so lamentably in fulfillment after you have tucked your plants into the soil. Still,
one hopes." Still, one hopes. I like that. Without an inex-
haustible reservoir of hope, gardeners would be inside drinking beer and watching TV.

Hope was surging on a Friday in May when I geared up
to make yet one more assault on my Everest of gardening.

I knew exactly what I wanted: a classic summer-perennial
bed. From years of fooling around with perennials in the border along the back lawn, I knew the ones that were hardiest, the
least temperamental, with the longest blooming season, whose

flowers were shades of yellow, blue, or white, whose textures and heights would work well together, the ones that come back even stronger the next year. I folded my wish list and carried it with me to work.

A new shipment must have arrived at the nursery in the morning, for when I got there after work, everything I wanted was waiting, big, beautiful, healthy, blooming specimens. Feeling like a game-show contestant with five minutes to take as much cash as possible out of a vault before the other contestants arrived, I filled up cart after cart with my selections: Russian sage with its misty haze of blue; golden coreopsis; low-growing daisies; Shasta daisies; the ethereal but steadfast moonbeam tickseed; moonshine yarrow with its flattened yellow flowers and lacy gray foliage; silver mound; blue campanula; white coneflowers; lavender; black-eyed Susans; the ever faithful veronica.

Rob watched in amazement as I wheeled the carts over to him. "Boy, someone's going to be busy this weekend!"

"I'm going for broke this time. This is it. I'm aiming for the perfect perennial garden."

"Well, you're getting the perfect plants. We can deliver those if you want, you know."

"Oh." I hadn't given any thought to logistics. I looked at the carts. I looked at my car. That sounded pretty good. "What time do you think they'd arrive?"

"Let's see. Tomorrow. Saturday." He pulled a small notebook out of his back pocket and flipped the pages. "I'd say sometime in the afternoon. Midafternoon, probably. How would that be?"

Midafternoon? "Maybe we could get them all in my car?"

Rob looked skeptical. "Well, let's give it a try and see what happens."

On the floor in front of the front seat. Plastic on the front seat, gallon containers on top. Jammed in two and three deep across the backseat. On the floor. In the trunk standing up, taller ones on their side. Every inch of space occupied by plants.

"See?" Rob said, shaking his head and carefully lowering the trunk. "No problem. Good luck!"

I climbed into my mobile greenhouse, fragrant with lavender and Russian sage and the wonderful smell of green, and drove slowly home.

That evening I laid out the plants on the terrace in front of the garden, spacing them just as they would be, arranging and rearranging until it got too dark. Then I waited for dawn.

By Saturday noon, an established perennial garden in full bloom graced my terrace garden, looking as if it had developed and filled in over the last twenty years. Of course, an instant perennial garden is the ultimate oxymoron, and the proof of it will depend on what happens in the years ahead.

From the terrace, go up the six stone steps that Pat and Tony put in years ago to replace the rotting railroad ties. Before we move on, take a look at the lawn.

Lawns have been getting a bad rap of late, and maybe there is something a bit ridiculous about this curious crop of grass on which we lavish more acreage than any other, including wheat and corn, pouring on water, fertilizers, and chemicals to make it grow, only to cut it down and throw it away. But although it doesn't feed our stomachs, there is something about a lawn that does feed our souls and, in the bargain, sets off the beauty of a garden and brings tranquillity to a landscape. It's always been that way. "Nothing," wrote Francis Bacon, "is more pleasing to the eye than green grass kept finely shorn."

I love everything about a lawn, the way the first warm spring rain brings it to life overnight after winter, the rhythmic movement of a water sprinkler, the sound of a lawn mower, certainly the whir of the old hand mowers but also from inside a classroom the hypnotic hum of a power mower, louder and softer, moving back and forth across the playing fields, the perfect look of a lawn with the brush strokes of the mowing lines just after it's been cut, the smell of cut grass in June and the smell of the grass of a playing field as it mingles with the sharp stone smell of a cinder track baking in the sun, the smell of the lawn after autumn leaves have been raked and the trampled grass smell of a football field, the smell of a box of grass seed when you open it, the translucent green of a garden hose, the new green of the lawn in spring, the contrast of a yellow dandelion, teasing out a blade of grass as you listen during a class outside under the trees, the feel of a beautiful lawn on bare feet, the sensuous look of a pile of fresh grass clippings like a small Cézanne haystack you can thrust your hands into and toss into the air, how after a long hot summer a half inch of rain and the cooler nights of September turn the grass electric green, and frosty November mornings when it's rimmed with white.

From the sunny lawn, go through the arbor onto the brick paths that meander under the shade of the oaks and lindens through the woodland wildflower gardens, past the old azaleas and laurel, rhododendron and andromeda, underplanted with masses of Virginia bluebells and blue phlox, blue wood hyacinths and blue hardy geraniums, lilies of the valley and violets, jacks-in-the-pulpit and mayapples and lady's slippers. You'll see in shady nooks ancestors of the earth's oldest plants—the ferns—maidenhair fern and ladyfern and ostrich fern, Japanese fern, cinnamon fern, and Christmas fern. You'll pass island beds of hosta with white variegated leaves, and textured blue-gray leaves large as elephant ears, and greenish-gold leaves edged in deep green, and heart-shaped leaves and corrugated leaves. I've been carving this woodland garden out of weeds and brambles and briers and thickets, opening vistas, creating focal points, continuing the paths. Now as lush and overgrown as a private Charleston garden, it's survival of the fittest here until I'm finally forced to cut back a little or pull out. Back in there, hidden away among the trees, is the cedar gazebo weathered silver, just big enough for a tiny Parisian café table and two chairs, and beyond it, the small sunny bed bordered by boxwood and filled with impatiens in a design like a Persian carpet.

You can walk through this secret garden whenever you want. You can sit in the gazebo or on the teak bench way back under the big oak, hidden from the world, and watch the sunlight and shadows move on the leaves. You can draw a deep breath and listen to what the breeze in the tops of the trees is trying to tell you. After a while you'll begin to wallow in the wonder of the moment, which, you somehow understand, is really all we can count on and all we have and all we need. Before long you'll feel as refreshed, as relaxed, as if you've been away on vacation. When you know a garden well, there is so much to see, so much to ponder and anticipate, that there is nowhere else you would rather be. Said Jefferson of his mountaintop home, "All my wishes end, where I hope my days will end, at Monticello." It's like the Paris

Hemingway wrote about: "We always returned to it no matter who we were or how it was changed or with what difficulties, or ease, it could be reached. Paris was always worth it." So, too, you can return to a garden when you know it by heart, whenever you need to, wherever you may happen to be, when your teeth are being drilled or when you wait outside an operating room or as you sit through an interminable meeting, and as your mind wanders along the familiar old brick paths, you can feel the same serenity as if you were there.

## II

INSECTS SHRILL through drowsy summer afternoons.

Days dream to dusk.

And night comes slowly.

It is the steps of a family out for a walk after supper. The evening smell of the grass when it's almost too dark to see the bushes along the back of the yard. Fireflies in the garden. The thrush's vesper call somewhere in the woods across the road. Voices from the softball game down at the field that stop, too. And after a while the sound of the insects in the trees in the night, rising and falling, humming, droning on and on as they did long ago for Pliny, they "never ceaseth all night long," maybe maybe maybe, on and on as you sleep, world without end, amen. Amen.

# III

GERTRUDE JEKYLL drew a distinction between what she called "commonplace gardening and gardening that may rightly claim to rank as a fine art." Whether a gardener is just having some fun or is intent on creating fine art, the work of the gardener seems exponentially more difficult than the work of other artists. Perhaps therein lies part of the challenge and allure, for the rules of the game keep changing, and the medium in which the gardener works is so much more evanescent than the painter's or the writer's, the sculptor's or the architect's. The gardener's easel is not static like a canvas or a page, a block of stone or a building, but rather is ever changing. Without the constant fiddling of the gardener on his work of art, it simply ceases to exist. It's as if David's abs would prolapse if Michelangelo weren't there chipping away at the marble every few days, or as if Mona Lisa's smile would turn into a hag's scowl if Leonardo da Vinci weren't continually touching up the canvas. Gardening is trying to create something that looks permanent on a canvas that twists and turns, rips and stretches and changes consistency.

Even as the gardener works at his masterpiece, forces beyond his control are conspiring to ruin it.

It all starts with a two-week summer vacation in July, which the gardens seem to regard just as all teenagers would a two-week absence of their parents: P-A-R-T-Y!

While I'm away, I picture the gardens going about their daily chores and saying their prayers in the evening, the sprinkler system coming on every Sunday, Tuesday, and Thursday morning at six o'clock, the shrubs and flowers following all the sensible rules and regulations I've established and taught them, all happily maintaining their best appearance through good, clean living. What I encounter when I return—the equivalent of a house strewn with beer cans and wine bottles, cigarette butts, crusty pizza boxes, condoms, and underwear—makes me suspect the worst: that what really goes on while I'm gone are scenes straight out of *Risky Business,* in which a teenage Tom Cruise ran a brothel out of his house while his parents were away.

The lilies, so prim and proper when I left them, look like a prom queen crawling on her hands and knees out from under the stadium bleachers, her gown twisted about her waist, her once golden blossoms worn and frazzled. The coreopsis I had carefully staked are now sprawled over the ground, listless after all the debauchery, in desperate need of deadheading. Pachysandra is disobeying orders and venturing out onto the forbidden brick paths; forsythia is reaching to grope and fondle anything green; honeysuckle, not so choosy, is caught in the act of cross-species coupling, which the law would classify as a crime against nature; and rabbits, who crashed the party, have deflowered every dianthus.

There have been orgies of growth, everyone has stayed up way past their bedtime, their eyes are bloodshot, they've eaten nothing but junk food, gone off their exercise programs, had way too much to drink, maybe even smoked some of the funny stuff if it was offered to them, and goodness knows, there were enough uninvited guests to bring every conceivable controlled dangerous substance and communicable disease. There's cocky crabgrass growing high between the lilies and hiding low, crawling over the soil around the impatiens by the road. Succulent weeds, 99 percent water, are trying to pass themselves off as part of the garden. Weeds with fierce thorns that frighten even the toughest bouncer have sprung up everywhere and are twisting themselves around their hostesses. (How do these weeds grow ten or twelve inches in two weeks? Maybe that's no sweat, if bamboo can grow three feet in twenty-four hours.) The sassafras clearly has been making whoopee; there are babies already poking up through the soil. The ash, too, bigtime. Chickweed, plantains, dandelions, clover: all have defiled the lawn, which, no longer putting-green perfect but trampled, thatchy, rather looks like it served as the disco floor for the party.

Exactly when does all this happen? What would I find if I made an unexpected return during those two weeks? I'm inclined to regard what I do in the gardens as nothing more than lollygagging, tweaking a little here and there as I wander around, nothing very serious, nothing very strenuous, rarely anything purposeful; though maybe it's just that, the constant tweaking, that keeps a garden from going feral. Or maybe all gardens need is some adult supervision. Oh, all the plants are quite contrite when I drive up the driveway and take an astonished look around, but they all need an aspirin and a cold compress, Band-Aids and a touch of iodine dabbed on as they bravely wince, a pat and a long nap.

Just when is it, for instance, that those creepy vines lurking behind my neighbor's garage decide to make their move and jump the five or six feet of open air between the tree and my hedge of forsythia? How do they even know the forsythia is there to grasp? Are they like that deformed nightmare the blind man Pew in *Treasure Island,* tap-tap-tapping down the frozen road with his cane until young Jim Hawkins at the Admiral Benbow held out his hand to help "and the horrible, soft-spoken, eyeless creature gripped it in a moment like a vice"? So the naive forsythia, perhaps offering to help those wayward waving tendrils, or perhaps excited by a walk on the wild side, holds out a branch and so is squeezed in a death grip until it is impossible to pull the vines off without ripping out the forsythia.

There must be a time when this happens, when, if you happened to be standing right there watching, you would see the tendrils groping, searching for a victim to embrace, to strangle as with a silk stocking about the neck. What nights there are out here, what strange happenings go on while we're away or lay asleep, what spectacles to behold.

Dusk is when the gangs begin to gather.

Through the darkening sky, bats climb and swoop in the erratic flight pattern of rabid birds, as if staying aloft is dependent on a tightly wound rubber band, just like those balsa airplanes we played with as children down at Memorial Field. Suddenly they're buzzing in at you. Are there insects around the porch light, is that what they're after? Are there insects around your head? What do they want? Why are they coming in so close? Inside seems a better spot in which to contemplate these questions.

The security lights at the back of the house snap on. I peep out around the kitchen-door curtain to see what triggered them. Crawling along the lawn, nosing here and there, is an opossum with its pink nose and hairless tail, a frightful little creature, grunting and snorting as if to discharge a troublesome hunk of impacted mucus from its nostrils, poking along the base of the stone wall, then passing into the shadows beyond the beam of light.

Why is it that the cute animals are out during the day, whereas the truly hideous ones come out only in the dark of night? We watch in fascination the antics of a chipmunk frolicking along the top of the wall and toss nuts to it; a rat's head peering out from between the rocks would horrify us. Squirrels are presentable and enliven the landscape; flying squirrels know enough not to show themselves. Why would an opossum even consider coming out during the day to be met with gasps of alarm and cries of horror? How many times could you take that before realizing it's better to do your shopping late at night? Could animal behavior be conditioned by the responses of other animals? Very young babies have been found to gravitate toward good-looking adults; do animals have some sense of their own looks and the looks of other animals? The blue jay acts as insufferably proud of its crest as a teenage boy of his slicked-up pompadour; if it could stand in front of a mirror all day combing it, that's what it would most like to be doing. Bats know they are too ugly to be abroad in daylight.

"I believe," Thoreau noted, "that men are generally still a little afraid of the dark, though the witches are all hung, and Christianity and candles have been introduced." A little? Ye gods, Henry, did you ever walk around Walden at night? Of course we're afraid. And with good reason.

If a garden ever is ours at all, it is only during the daylight hours. Never at night.

The nights are laced with horror.

The haunted hoot of the great horned owl echoes eerily in the treetops, too close for comfort, and I bet cocky br'er rabbit, who nibbles the clover in my back lawn all day long, scared of nothing and certainly not of me, is hiding in bed under the covers, just like I am, listening, glad to be in for the night. "Who who? Who? Who?" owl demands. Who will be owl's supper tonight? Who indeed.

Not twenty feet from my open bedroom window, the warm summer midnight is ripped open with snarls and bloody screams of raccoons intent on either murdering each other or having some really incredible sex. Feet pound across the roof in chase and escape. Something crashes through the woods across the road, sounding like the midnight ride of the headless horseman. The security lights out back are tripped by something passing by. I consider getting out of bed to peek from behind the drapes, but then roll over and pull the sheet up higher. I'd rather not know. Like Jim Hawkins and his mother, all we can do is cower and tremble under the bridge beyond the old Admiral Benbow, cower and tremble and pray for morning.

Morning, a sunny morning, and all is serene. But sometimes there's evidence that the nightmares were real. Snails lie dead on the bricks around the pool. Like a burglar's muddy footprints along the carpet down the back hall, indistinguishable prints trample through the orderly bed of red, pink, and white begonias, haphazardly crushing them. A neighbor's trap, with a dead groundhog in it, has made its way through? under? over? my deer fence and clear across my yard. A clump of hosta and fern is inexplicably smashed down, with no other signs of damage: what landed on them with a sickening thud?

As I fill the birdbath, my groggy eyes catch something out of place. On the flagstone step by the birdbath, right next to my feet. A dead bird? No, a squirrel. On its back. Its feet in the air. Its head bent to the side at a crazy angle. Its round gray tummy split open lengthwise, bloody guts hanging out from the gash. I step back in shock and stare. What happened? What story of surprise attack could this scene tell?

What to do? A shovel. I'll get a shovel and dispose of it. But the thought of lifting it and carrying it down the driveway and across the road, balancing it on the blade, trying to keep it from slip-sliding off until I can toss it down the ridge, makes my arms feel like Thanksgiving's jellied cranberry sauce. What are vultures for, anyway? And where are they? I look high up in the sky like folks do in Westerns; they should know it's here by now, shouldn't they? What is this, they don't start work until after nine o'clock? Are there in fact vultures around here, or are they only out west? In movies? They're everywhere, aren't they? If not, wouldn't any self-respecting cat want to take this home, or a raccoon? At least the crows will come and pick it over when I'm at work.

But when I get home and remember to check, there it is, untouched. What am I supposed to say to these finicky scavengers: "May I wrap that for you?" Perhaps suburban scavengers have developed gourmet tastes. Okay, I'll take the easy way out and just avoid that part of the yard. But like a rubbernecker passing a highway crash, I can't help looking, even if from a distance. One day flies buzz around the gash. Another day the squirrel looks like it has stiffened. After a day of rain, it looks a lot worse for wear, but still no sign of carrion beetles to dispose of the corpse. And then, before the end of the week: gone. Has it just been dragged under the azaleas by the birdbath? Am I someday going to step on a half-eaten carcass? Gingerly I peer around. No sign of it. All clear. Is this how all the dead birds and animals go? Why we don't have stinking carcasses all over our yards? Like the dead hawk I found one morning on the terrace, do they just, like in a vanishing act in a magic show, disappear?

Now, a lot of what goes on at night may be attributable to teenage raccoons, which at best are brats, and at worst juvenile delinquents. Not even their mothers would dispute that.

They delight in overturning the two bronze geese under the rhododendron, just for the sport of it. I picture them racing into them at full speed to perfect their body blocks. On steamy summer nights they take a dip in the goldfish pool, and then, like teenagers who come out of the shower soaking wet and walk across the carpet, drip puddles across the terrace. (I attribute this to the teenage raccoons, since I've seen a family do it the proper way. One summer night when the back lights were tripped, curious and more awake than usual, I arose to see what was out there. A mother and father and three young raccoons were coming from a bath in the goldfish pool and walking single-file along the top of the terrace wall, taking special care not to step on any plants. When they got to the end of the wall, they jumped the two feet to the ground one after the other, and resumed their polite single-file formation. When the last, the littlest raccoon, came to the end of the wall, he looked down tentatively, doubtfully, like a first-time high-board diver, watched his family resuming its procession, looked down again, and thinking better of a jump, turned, held on to the vine dangling over the edge of the wall, and shinned himself down hand over hand, looking over his shoulder to gauge how far it was to the ground, then, lickety-split, ran to catch up with the others.) No, it's the teenagers who get into all the trouble. On a whim, they decide to scoop the snails out of the goldfish pool and leave them lying there on the bricks to die; they don't eat them or take them home, it's just wanton mischief. They rip open the container of fish food kept behind the boxwood by the pool and gorge on all of it. They topple over the fountain in the pool and pull the plastic tubing askew. When they feel like it, they help themselves to fat goldfish, boning some, leaving others lying on the terrace, and still others out on the middle of the lawn. On collection days, they pry open the garbage cans on the driveway, peer in, and strew the week's garbage helter-skelter to get at the chicken bones. No, not even their mothers have anything good to say about them.

But not everything that happens at night can be blamed on raccoons. There are still enough inexplicable events so that the wise gardener confines gardening expeditions to the safe hours between dawn and dusk. The rest is better left to the gangs.

# IV

SOME OF THE GANGS can play pretty rough, and they don't play fair.

How hard is it to go to the nursery, buy a flat or two of marigolds, plant them in the well-prepared soil of a sunny bed, water them, and sit back to enjoy them for the rest of the season? Marigolds have always been a favorite of mine, and I started out with them years ago. Was that asking too much? Gardening doesn't get much simpler; any gas station can pull it off with flair.

For a week the marigolds perform as expected, but then, though still blooming merrily, they don't seem to be growing. No new leaves, no new buds. A shot of Miracle-Gro should fix that up, you think. But it doesn't. They still look weak, stunted. Was there, you wonder in a haze of inexperience, something wrong with those particular flats? Back to the nursery, buy some more, throw out the first crop, and plant the next. Within a week or two, you encounter the same results. And then one fine day you take a close look at the pitiful plants and see it, a sniveling slug on the underside of a leaf. It's been chewing the leaves to shreds, you can see that now, snapping the stems, snipping the flowers, sucking out their lifeblood. In your anger, you momentarily put aside your revulsion and pull off that hideous little hunk of snot, stomp it on the driveway, annihilate it beyond recognition, try to wipe its mucus trail from your fingers, and go back to make sure it didn't have any colleagues waiting around for it. Colleagues? Now that you know what you're looking for, it's like a scene straight out of *West Side Story*, where someone whistles and a gang materializes out of every doorway and alley, ready to rumble. They're on every marigold.

Sink a tuna can into the soil, your gardening friends advise you, fill it with beer, and the slugs will drop by for a drink after work and drown. Put out a grapefruit rind, others say, and pick it up in the morning to find it covered with them. No, no, eggshells, crushed eggshells, they're the ticket; spread them around the plants, since the slugs can't stand crawling over them, it must tickle their bellies. Sprinkle just a touch of salt on them and they dissolve, pfffff! Copper strips laid around the plants will give them a nasty electric jolt as they slime over them. Pick them off in the evening or early morning and drop them into a can filled with Clorox or Wisk.

Each form of capital punishment works, but the slugs are working faster, each producing some five hundred slug eggs. So unless you have nothing else to do but be a bartender for your slugs, you quickly learn you must turn to chemical warfare and sprinkle slug bait around their preferred dishes, repeating the dose after every rain; perhaps, for good measure, setting an example each week by publicly torturing a couple. One of my favorite images is of my grandmother dressed in her summer garden dress and straw hat, with two gloved fingers picking a slug from a lily in her sunken garden and, with fancy gardening shears that looked like they were meant to cut bouquets of sweet peas, snipping the slug in half and watching in grim satisfaction as its green innards oozed out.

Spotting some of the other gangs is a little like seeing a

panzer division on maneuvers in your backyard: you know it's going to do a lot of damage, you know you have to get it out of there fast, but you're not quite sure how.

Some years ago the extension of a highway through a part of the Watchung Reservation upset the herds of deer living there and drove them out to the promised land of suburbia. It was quite a novelty to see a group of deer stroll down the road in the evening, leisurely looking around like any family out for an after-dinner walk, almost nodding as they passed by. Some mornings I'd awaken to find twelve or fifteen deer curled up sound asleep on the back lawn. The novelty wore off quickly when I discovered that my guests' appetites were insatiable and that my gardens had become their personal salad bar, that my azaleas, my rhododendron, my hosta, my laurel, my arborvitae, in fact pretty much everything I had lugged home from the nursery and planted and nurtured was to them like a bowlful of bacon bits. Dinners were never this delicious or this convenient in the forest.

Deer don't have a reputation for bravery, so it seemed a rather simple matter to let them know they had overstayed their welcome. On a frozen winter day as they munched on azaleas, I stood at the back door in deerskin gloves and threw at them my only ready projectiles—lemons—which they watched with quite a bit of interest as each landed just short or just far of some deer ass. They looked at me, looked down at the lemons, and likely wondered why I wasn't squeezing them onto their salad; obviously anyone with an ounce of sense would know how hard this would be to do with cloven hooves. What kind of host was I, anyway, they seemed to ask. Waving my deerskin-gloved hands and shouting, "See what could happen to you!," I chased them into my neighbor's yard, a chase that could have been spliced into a Disney film as they leaped gracefully, playfully, ahead, looked back to see how I was doing, took a few more leaps, then waited for me to chug along and almost catch up. They weren't taking this seriously at all, and I certainly hadn't conveyed the message that they really were no longer welcome as guests, for back they came as soon as I went indoors. They probably found the chase an amusing diversion from their usual routine of nibble and nap, nibble and nap. The clatter of aluminum pie plates strung around their favorite bushes, bars of soap pierced and hung from branches, sprays guaranteed to repel them: I tried them all, but as with Edward Gorey's Doubtful Guest, there was no getting rid of them.

The time must come for every gardener to decide between a yard planted with daffodils and andromeda, just about the only two plants deer regard as distasteful as brussels sprouts, and a yard planted with exactly what one wants to grow. A deer fence around the property—black vinyl mesh material, all but invisible unless you're right on top of it, that blends in with the perimeter plantings of forsythia, spruce, hemlock, lilac, and holly—did the trick. In fact, it is so invisible that the deer couldn't see it and crashed right through the first day it was up. White ribbons tied at varying heights let them know it was there until they learned new routes to more open-minded neighborhood restaurants.

Even after years of deer war, I can still recognize the beauty and grace of these animals. I can acknowledge (to myself, at least; not to them) their rights to this piece of land, which may well have been part of their ancestral ranging grounds even before the Indians camped in the valley between the Watchung ridges. I have no problem sharing my suburban lot with all the others who make it their home or hotel or restaurant—squirrels and skunks, raccoons, possums, bats and hawks, robins and rabbits, chipmunks, crows and katydids, the cat that takes a siesta in the gazebo on hot summer afternoons, and the big old wild turkey that waddles around for a look now and then. I'll even lend them a hand when they need it, staying clear of a poorly sited robin's nest, rescuing a cicada fluttering helplessly in the garden pool, keeping the birdbath clean and filled with fresh water, providing food when the winters are hard, distracting the neighbor's cat as it stalks a chipmunk. But I draw the line at groundhogs. Groundhogs are the enemy.

My first reaction to a groundhog sighting is identical to that of the countries surrounding Nazi Germany when they noticed Hitler's war machine gathering at their borders: denial. Denial, denial, denial. The hosta that has been mysteriously stripped of every leaf, that can be explained away. The rotund rump of a big fat mama groundhog scurrying through the pachysandra and across the road into the woods, well, that's where she belongs, in the woods; she'll know not to come across the road again. The groundhog grazing on the lawn on a sunny afternoon, a peaceful scene, and it doesn't seem to harm the grass; maybe it's as good as sheep trimming it. Let it be. A groundhog on its hind legs, eyeing the clematis growing over the arbor; a clap of the hands and it scoots away.

And then one day I step outside and come face-to-face with a baby groundhog on the terrace, not ten feet away. It freezes. I do, too. And think. Perfect time for some behavior modification. The hose is right there. Slowly I lean over and pick it up. The baby groundhog, too frightened to move, stares at me, trembling. Okay, here's a little lesson to report back to your mom and dad. I turn the faucet on full blast and spray it. Bull's-eye! In a moment it regains its senses and takes off with me in hot pursuit, hosing it down as it races up along the rock wall and disappears into the greenery behind the new perennial garden. It must have gone into a neighbor's yard. Where it must live. Where it belongs. That family won't be back visiting anytime soon.

Oh, yeah? The hose lesson seems to have been for naught. It turns out that groundhogs must like water as much as br'er rabbit liked the brier patch. The next humid afternoon, a groundhog sits in the middle of the back lawn as the sprinkler system swirls around him, shakes himself off after it passes, watches as it circles around and comes back to sprinkle him again, shakes once more, cooling off on a sweltering afternoon. He'll have to tell his friends about the neighborhood amusement park.

One afternoon, again admiring the new perennial garden, I notice that the black-eyed Susans in the back border seem to be moving a little, rustling, even though there's no breeze. As I step closer to take a look, out darts a groundhog heading, as always, in the same direction, above the stone wall into the greenery. On inspection, I see that all the leaves on a few of the stems of the black-eyed Susans have been stripped.

This is the day neutrality ends and war is declared. I get some black mesh webbing and stake it around the black-eyed Susans to protect them. The next day, the cone flowers next to the black-eyed Susans are devoid of every leaf, with just the white flower left atop the stem, almost in spite. They don't look half as good that way. Out comes the deer repellent and every plant in the garden is sprayed, the spray so vile I can taste it and smell it for a day. But it doesn't deter the groundhog, which has now moved on to the campanula, eating those delicate plants right down to the dirt, followed by a dessert of daisies.

The groundhog escape route leads me to the door of its den, along the border under the pines, cleverly hidden in a bed of pachysandra, with just a tiny telltale pile of fresh clay right outside the front door. What would any good Elmer Fudd do when confronted by such a frustrating adversary? Assemble the home arsenal of conventional weapons. How about pouring a bottle of ammonia into the hole? That's a start. Then follow up with a box of mothballs, the kind with the warning that if you happen to inhale by mistake, call 911 immediately, and then, if you're still conscious, try to hit the speed dial for the Poison Control Center in Atlanta, since there won't be time for the paramedics to get there. Shove those little suckers way back in there, that's right. Wait: aren't there warnings about the deadly gas formed by mixing ammonia and Clorox? Okay, pour in the Clorox, too. Then seal up that door with some large rocks, pack them right in real tight. And as Captain Hook taught us, how about a special treat left right outside the front door? The groundhog's favorite delicacy, sliced apples, mixed in with a more than generous helping of rat poison. (They say that fox, coyote, bobcat, or wolf urine sprinkled around the plants will keep groundhogs away, but if you're the kind of person who can assist a fox, coyote, bobcat, or wolf in squirting where you want it to or, alternatively, urinating neatly into a bottle, getting rid of a mere groundhog is not going to present you a problem.) And voilà, the days of wine and roses, Mr. Groundhog, are o-v-e-r.

Until tomorrow. When he's back in business as if nothing happened. Unlike Rasputin after he ate those poison cakes and drank the poisoned wine, he's not even stumbling.

There he is, sitting at the entrance to his home, staring at me. Right at me. The enemy has been met. The battle lines are drawn. I remember reading in *Reader's Digest* what to do if you're walking in the woods and all of a sudden confront a grizzly: motion with your arms and body to make yourself appear bigger than you are. This same tactic should scare the bejesus out of a groundhog. I raise my hands over my head and stand on my toes and stare straight at him, hissing. He sits there staring at me, as if watching a carnival freak show, and all but claps for an encore. I raise my arms again, even wider, even higher, and this time, staring at him, I growl. No reaction whatsoever. I wonder if it would work any better with a grizzly, or if this is one of those bits of lore—like if you're attacked by an alligator, try to cover its eyes; right, no problem—that could never, ever be implemented. I do know this: if the groundhog had tried the equivalent groundhog threat, maybe snarling and baring his teeth or feinting a lunge in my direction to see what

I'd do, I'd be inside the kitchen with the door bolted quicker than he could summon his friends to watch.

Concluding that it's time to call in a trapper is just about as hard a decision to reach as deciding to drop the bomb. The innocent will suffer as well as the guilty (and deep down inside, you really don't want the guilty to suffer, you just want them to move over to your neighbors). Into the trap, following the irresistible trail of apple, come raccoons, squirrels, possums, and an occasional neighborhood cat, and you avoid the yard as much as possible when the trapper, who could have had a role in *Deliverance,* arrives and goes to work. As frightened and appealing and pleading as the groundhog now looks in the trap when you get home from work ("I told you this would happen," you tell him as you slip a carrot into the trap in case he's hungry), you're relieved that the battle is over at last. The trapper chuckles when he arrives the next morning; where there's one, he explains patiently as if to a city slicker, there is a family. And so the trapping continues, day after day (after the first easy catch, they seem wary, and the trap must be relocated again and again around their haunts, with apple smeared over any parts touched by human hands and apple trails luring them in), until the mother and father and four children are caught and taken away in his ominous truck; where, you don't ask, and would rather not know.

Suddenly the yard seems too quiet, lifeless, without a chubby groundhog grazing in the grass and scurrying for cover when you pass by a window inside the house. Holden Caulfield was right: after a while you sort of miss everybody, even the enemy.

## V

THE DROUGHT IS NEXT.

It begins just as *The Grapes of Wrath* began, with the blue days of June and day after day of sunshine. Then comes July with mornings when you wake and the temperature is in the high seventies and into the eighties within an hour of sunrise, 98, 99, 100, 102 by noon, so stifling that when you leave the air-conditioned office to go out for lunch, your eyeballs feel like they'll dry up as you cross the parking lot. The lawns around the office park become less green and stop growing and turn to stubble, and the begonias in the beds along the walkways fade, and the rhododendron leaves curl and then brown and drop off. At home you increase the cycle of the underground sprinkler system from three times a week to every other day, to every day, to—and you feel guilty about this after the voluntary watering restrictions are announced—morning and evening, and you're maintaining everything but not gaining any ground, nothing seems happy, the lawn is green but thin, patchy, parched-looking, browning around the edges where the sprinkler's spray is weaker, and the crabgrass and clover are moving in. The impatiens along the wall down by the road are bravely blooming, but their foliage looks tired, and even the inde-structible independent barberry, weary and dusty, seems to be calling for a helping hand. Each evening you fill the watering can again and again and carry it down to them. Wherever you look is an emergency: the andromeda at the end of the brick path is shriveling; as you let the hose soak the soil around it for a while, you notice that the azaleas out-side the sunroom look like they're in their last hour. You spot a dead branch on a mock orange that's been happily grow-ing for over forty years in the back corner of the yard and realize it's not just one dead branch but the entire shrub. You water and water, ninety-one thousand gallons in the two weeks since you returned from vacation, and keep watering, knowing what's coming.

Every headline announces it: DROUGHT EMERGENCY DECLARED. Neighbors are encouraged to turn in neighbors using sprinklers. Police cars cruise the streets looking for tell-tale puddles, a suspiciously green lawn, ready to make a pub-lic example of the first violator they catch. (Imagine the headlines in the local paper: RESIDENT WATERS LAWN ILLE-

GALLY WHILE NEIGHBORHOOD CHILDREN GO WITHOUT BATHS. Picture the two photos they would run: you looking out over your greensward, a smug supercilious smile of satisfaction caught by the telephoto lens; a group of neighborhood urchins, wide-eyed, filthy, pitiful.) At least you can still water with a hose, as long as you're holding it, and you resolve to spend as much time doing that as you must. But after the first ten minutes it begins to get tiresome, and as you drag the hose from victim to victim—"Hang on, hang on," you tell them as you let the cool water gush between their parched lips and swollen tongues and they settle back to rest—you are overwhelmed by how much must be done to keep a small yard alive. The very next morning you hear them calling again, "Water! water!"

You begin better to understand how nurses in the makeshift Civil War hospitals must have felt after battle: roomfuls of wounded soldiers moaning, begging for help, everybody calling for water, Please! Help me! Maybe you could help the one who was only grazed by a musket ball, but there wasn't the time or the medical staff or the supplies to help everyone, so you went from cot to cot, doing what little you could to ease their misery, offering a quiet word of encouragement, a pat on the brow, as you became more discouraged, more resigned to the fact that there really was nothing you could do to help, that despite your best inten-

tions, your best efforts, there would indeed be casualties, soldiers dead and crippled and horribly maimed, and that as
much as you wanted to help, bottom line, it would be the
strong and the lucky who survived.

The rhododendrons curl up their leaves and droop, the
forsythia withers, the azaleas expire overnight, the spruce
and the pines try to be strong for the others, standing tall and
green, but if you go over and examine these stoics, you'll see
they are losing needles and brown wither is traveling up the
green. The viburnums have gone into shock, the dogwoods
are faint, the pachysandra has keeled over. You go from
emergency to emergency pulling the hose like an oxygen
mask that you hold over their faces as you perform CPR.
One and two, breathe! breathe! and as soon as you get a
pulse, you're on to the next.

What have you done? You've bought them another
twenty-four hours, more or less, another day of life, and like
the farmers in the dust bowl, you scan the sky and watch as
clouds build up and mass together and turn gray and the sky
darkens and distant thunder rumbles, come on! Come on!
Sometimes a few drops splatter here and there, or a shower
starts and immediately stops so that the terrace is dry ten
minutes later, and the clouds slip apart and the sun shines
through and it's hotter and more humid than it was before,
and the heat beats down and the days burn on and the earth

rushes through space, closer to the sun. "The clouds appeared," Steinbeck wrote, "and went away, and in a while they did not try any more."

But you watch the clouds anyway and listen to the long-range forecasts. A robin squats in the birdbath, spreads its wings open, and stays there like that, like a child in a wading pool, until a blue jay harries it out and takes its place. The begonias in the office park stop growing and just stand there startled, and even the weeds weaken and go limp and fall over onto the soil. The next day is just the same, with the sun and the heat sucking out whatever moisture remains in anything green. So you're out there like the *Baywatch* lifeguards, and each day the victims become weaker and weaker, their ability to snap back after the water transfusions becomes slower and slower and, ultimately, their chances of survival less and less. The power to save them all is yours, you know that. All you have to do is flip on that switch in the basement and let the sprinkler run and run until they're satiated and the soil is as soggy as after a downpour and the water is dribbling down their chins. But you can't. You can't save them. It's against the law, and it would be wrong, that's for sure. Maybe it's time to remember that last line in Robert Frost's poem "Good-by and Keep Cold," the poem about thinking of the orchard at the far edge of the farm, of everything the winter can do to harm next year's crop, but the narrator has done all he can to safeguard his trees, and the poem closes with "But something has to be left to God." Still, the power to save everything in your yard is yours, you know that. It's in your hands. God is busy enough. One flip of a switch.

The penalties are steep, very steep—$500 for the first offense, $1,000 for every offense thereafter, and community service? Jail time? The pillory? But how much will it cost to replace what you're losing? How do you put a price on mature plantings? Where would you even go to replace them? Okay, what would it cost to buy ninety-one thousand gallons of Poland Spring water? That's an awful lot of jugs. How would you get them home from the supermarket? Fifty would be a carload, probably, and here we're talking ninety-one thousand just to hold ground for another two to three weeks? No, it's not a practical solution, but still, heat-dazed, you don't dismiss it out of hand.

Well, assume worse comes to worst, and one fine day there's a knock on your door and on the front porch are two police officers, summons pad in hand, handcuffs hanging from belts, the cruiser in the driveway with lights flashing.

"Hi, Officers," you say in your most innocent voice as you open the door, "may I help you?"

"This your home?"

"Yes, it is." You smile, still innocently.

"That's some lawn you have," the senior officer says,

admiring it as the other stares straight at you to catch a flinch.

"Thank you!" you say politely, just as your mother taught you.

"Look how green it is," the officer says, continuing his sadistic little game, "compared to all your neighbors', it certainly is nice and green. You could almost call it lush, couldn't you? Look at that. Just how do you manage that? What's your little secret?"

Little secret? He thinks he's going to wrest a confession on the front doorstep just like that? Deny everything, that seems to work best. You wonder whether Johnnie Cochran would come to the phone if you called him right now. How would you find his number? Don't you get one call? They haven't even gotten to a reading of your Miranda rights; remember that, it could turn out to be grounds for appeal. In fact, this whole episode of police harassment may be ultra vires. Do they have a proper warrant? Deny it all. Remember, deny it.

"Oh," you explain as if it's the most obvious thing in the world, "it's all the trees." You look up at the green canopy admiringly. "The shade, you know. Keeps the sun off."

You can tell from their jaded expressions that they're not buying it.

"And the seed I used," you quickly add, even though your

mouth is as dry as your lawn was before you turned the system on full blast. "It's that special type that was supposed to be quite drought-resistant. Seems to be working well." You smile wanly. "Thank goodness, since this summer's been a real doozy, hasn't it?"

There are people who could pull this off with panache, but you're not one of them; you're not good at this at all. People always look at you skeptically even when you're telling the truth. The officers are now looking convinced not only that you've been illegally draining the public reservoirs, but that there very well may be a missing family's miscellaneous body parts wrapped in aluminum foil in your freezer.

Well, how about this: you just got back from vacation and hadn't heard there was a drought emergency. No, too many people have seen you in the last two weeks. No alibi witnesses. And you wouldn't do well at all with a lie-detector test; you'd be sweating profusely, shaking, quivering, even before they put the cuffs on; man, that needle would be jumping instantly all over the graph paper and pegging you in whatever category is way beyond criminally insane.

How about a more simple truth: that your system malfunctioned and somehow went on, that it's on the blink and you have to get it repaired pronto, before it happens again and more precious water is wasted. You can see their tired expressions; they've apparently heard that one too. The thought of being driven to the station to hear a lecture and watch a grainy filmstrip on good citizenship makes you cringe.

Maybe you're a sleepwalker. Yes, that's it, you were sleepwalking and turned on the system without even knowing it.

Amnesia. Has anyone really ever gotten amnesia other than on soap operas?

These are night thoughts, the scenarios you rehearse and rehash and wrestle with when you awaken again in the dark, the sweat-slick sheets twisted about you, your plants, your children, outside sighing, moaning, struggling in the oppressive heat. It's a little after one o'clock. From start to finish it would take the sprinkler system two and a half hours to do its job, to run through its whole cycle. One o'clock to maybe three-thirty. The darkest, deepest, best hours to commit a crime.

Again you hear their silent calls for you, like a child calling in the middle of the night for a glass of water. Without even thinking you get the flashlight, cupping its beam so no light shines through the windows, creep down to the basement, flip the manual switch for the sprinkler system, hurry back upstairs, and climb into bed so they can find you there, sound asleep.

Through the rustlings of the night, any novice serial killer would sleep a less troubled sleep. You hear the sprinkler heads in the backyard whirring around and around, each splash of water on a leaf or tree trunk as loud as a gunshot. You visualize your neighbors sitting bolt upright in bed: "What's that?" they ask themselves in amazement. You hear a car pass by and hold your breath lest the sprinklers in front come on. A galumph in the pipes when the system shifts from station to station sounds like a rap on the front door: "Hands up! Get out here! Now! I said now!"

You're up early, looking for any evidence that will have to be tampered with or destroyed. There is a suspicious out-of-place puddle where some of the water ran down the drive-way to the road, just where you don't want it. You could take a sponge down there—cleaning the street, if anyone asked— but it should dry up momentarily. That day none of your neighbors seem to be looking at you strangely, or shaking a finger at you, or making veiled references to wasting water; there are no police cars in your driveway when you get home from work that evening (you're prepared to circle the block and keep driving if there are), no summonses taped to the front door, no messages on your answering machine to report to the police station for questioning. So, not that night but the next, you're up again at one to let it run, and over the next week or two, as all criminals do, you're becoming a bit more brazen, a bit more careless, hitting the back gardens shortly after dusk, keeping everything alive enough, green enough, to hold on until the day of amnesty when the sky looks and smells like El Greco's *View of Toledo,* and it rains all night and the next day and the next as if it will rain forever.


# VI


GARDENING IS ALL ABOUT learning how to replace the irreplaceable. That magnificent eighty-foot blue spruce, the one in the corner of the garden around which you built the woodland garden pool and the tiny waterfall and tucked in all the plantings that had finally matured: a freak windstorm blows it over to rest its tip against the neighbor's roof. (How is this devastation different from Leo Tolstoy typing a first draft of *War and Peace* on his personal computer, which crashes without any backup?) The weeping willow you babied for its first several years, until it started filling out and filling in that part of the garden just as you imagined it would, catches the storm winds like a sail and is ripped out by the roots. The same tempest cantilevers half of a century-old double linden right smack through a stand of birch. A winter freeze plays havoc with the boxwood border you planted decades ago that finally is the right height. An ice storm splits a hemlock. Three days of rain in May ruin the azalea blossoms just as they start their three-week show. The drought in July and August makes the blossoms of the forsythia and laurel, the crab apple and pear, tiny and anemic the next spring. An errant groundhog eats every single Virginia bluebell bud the day before their much anticipated flowering. To create a garden, a gardener needs not only some skill but also a gambler's run of luck.

Mildews. Molds. Japanese beetles. Black spot. Aphids. Plagues. Pestilence. The enemy is at all the borders, and a deer fence and coyote urine are no more stalwart than the Maginot Line. Grubs tunnel underground to suck roots, crabgrass invades crawling on its belly, windborne parachutists land behind the lines and begin their assault, weed seeds hitchhike in on shoes and clothes. Scale infests oaks, hemlocks, and flowering cherry trees; inchworms, tent caterpillars, and gypsy moths chew on the leaves of shade trees and ornamentals; red spiders, mealybugs, and lacewing flies attack in the hot summer months; leaf miners go to work on the hollies and birch; fungi diseases attack crab apples, cherry trees, ash trees, and dogwoods. A certain amount of sucking and chewing is acceptable, but if given the chance, some of these gangs go overboard. In the course of a year or two, eight mature trees—every dogwood on my property—were wiped out by a borer before I even knew the enemy had landed. They had their binoculars trained on my hemlock border when I put them on my Most Wanted List and started practicing a style of vigilante justice that made the gunslingers of the Old West look like Cub Scouts at a jamboree.

Despite these losses and setbacks, like King Sisyphus, gardeners forever keep rolling that rock up the hill, convinced we are progressing toward the day it will stay in place up there and not roll back on us, the day our gardens will be just as we want them. Gardeners need not only that run of luck but a tolerance for ambiguity, as the rules of the game keep changing; also a stubborn streak of defiance, an ability to assess the latest damage, to learn from experience and try again. In retirement at Monticello, Jefferson wrote to a friend, "but though an old man I am but a young gardener." Every gardener is. Even Gertrude Jekyll. As she wrote: "Those who do not know are apt to think that hardy flower gardening of the best kind is easy. It is not easy at all. It has taken me half a lifetime merely to find out what is best, worth doing, and a good slice out of another half to puzzle out the ways of doing it." Maybe this is why Vita Sackville-West called gardening "the most rejuvenating of all occupations." When everything goes wrong, we're always looking ahead. As we wander the garden and muse, looking around at different times of day, in different light, from different angles, new ideas bubble to the surface, and suddenly something clicks as to just how to replace the irreplaceable. Somehow it always works. Most of the time it's even better.

But there comes a day late in the summer when we're

weary of battle and, even if not quite ready to wave the white flag of defeat, quite willing to negotiate a truce. The new perennial bed may not look as bad as Tara's gardens after the war, but all the black-eyed Susans and the coneflowers are bare stalks, the daisies and campanulas have been devoured, the silver mound didn't survive the drought. The lawn looks tired, matted, weak, waiting for the cool nights of September. The marigolds out front have held their own against the repeated invasions of slugs, but they are pretty pathetic specimens compared to those at the gas station and in front of the post office. Like a boil about to burst, the remnants of the groundhogs' old home, which they dug out like a steam shovel, uprooting hostas and casting out soil and clay and rock, pock the perennial bed along the border.

The great Gertrude Jekyll tells us how "the duty we owe to our gardens and to our own bettering in our gardens is to use the plants that they shall form beautiful pictures; and that, while delighting our eyes they should be always training those eyes to a more exalted criticism; to a state of mind and artistic conscience that will not tolerate a bad or careless combination or any sort of misuse of plants, but in which it becomes a point of honor to be always striving for the best." That's all well and good, but right about now, late in August, we're satisfied with anything that's growing, whether or not it's the best. Our gardening goal of an orchestrated display of continuous bloom from the opening notes of early spring to the cymbal crash of first frost, so that the gardens appear to flower all season with seamless set changes between scenes, is a misty memory. Now we understand just what Thoreau wrote in his journal about how "the youth gets together his materials to build a bridge to the moon, or, perchance, a palace or temple on the earth, and, at length, the middle-aged man concludes to build a woodshed with them." At the end of the summer, battle-weary and bowed even if not broken, we've learned the woodshed of our garden will have to do.

# VII

LATE AUGUST, the ragged end of the season, and the garden is overgrown, frowsy, weary. It doesn't care anymore, and we don't, either. It's too hot to care and too humid to do anything even if we did. We gave up deadheading weeks ago and now, if anything, indiscriminately slash back dead and dying flowers, yellowing leaves, spindly stalks, glad to be through with them.

Late August, we stand and look back at what wasn't done. In April we looked ahead to everything we wanted to accomplish. Now all we can see is what didn't work out.

Late August, the stationery store in town is stocked with

school supplies, the blue three-ring notebooks and neat sheaves of lined paper, piles of index cards, pink erasers, mysterious protractors and compasses, ballpoint pens, colored dividers, and though they're not for us anymore, they signal the onset of E. B. White's "end-of-summer sadness" as surely as the late afternoon sun hitting the tallest trees on the far ridge across the valley.

Late August, and it's dark when we're still at the dinner table, too dark now for after-dinner walks. Now we read and go to bed earlier, while the field crickets and katydids, like the *Titanic*'s band on the aft deck, tick off the seconds till summer's end.

❀   ❀   ❀

Anyone can create a garden that looks good in the spring. The hard part is to keep it looking good throughout the summer and as far into the fall as possible. These are the seasons that separate the new recruits from grizzled veterans.

Someone once said that nature abhors a garden. A gardener will find continuing evidence to support this aphorism. How quickly an untended garden goes feral bears a startling inverse relationship to how long it took to create it.

Behind every spectacular garden is not only a lot of hard work, the right conditions, and luck, but also a bagful of tricks. Each plant, for instance, can be touched up—the dead and yellowing leaves clipped off, the plant shaped to perfection—and each group of plants structured as if in a painting. Annuals can be tucked in with perennials to extend the color range and season. If positioned properly, some plants can brace up others that otherwise would have to be staked.

Be realistic about your garden ideal. Just as a model doesn't look anything like what you see in the fashion pages if you happen to bump into her or him in the supermarket, so a garden bears little resemblance to what you see in a magazine or on a garden tour without a flurry of work beforehand.

# September Song

# I

TIME STOPS at the end of a season. For just a moment it stands still, suspended before everything starts to change again.

Summer's shadow across the lawn. Children walking September streets to school. A moment suspended, motionless in time, so quiet you can hear a leaf spiral through blue sky, the thud of an acorn falling on green grass.

It all happens, of course, when we're not watching, trees turning color, children growing up, parents growing older, seasons changing, years passing.

Blue sky and green grass, day after day, the football days of fall. Now the garden, ragged from the summer, can be trimmed and tidied up; the leaves that have been nibbled and chewed, sucked and scarred, cut back; the flimsy shoots and branches, pruned. Revived, the marigold blossoms have never looked so yellow, the ageratum so blue, the begonias and impatiens so white. With renewed vigor (could the pruning by the groundhogs have helped?), the black-eyed Susans burst onto center stage in the perennial garden, aiming to steal the show, backed up by the quiet chorus line of the white-flowered, sweet-scented hosta Aphrodite.

At the nursery, the wooden tables out by the road already are covered with pots of mums, golden and russet in bud and bloom, even though it doesn't feel like autumn. In the shed, bushel baskets overflow with bulbs, the dependable daffodils, the smooth tulip bulbs that once sparked such a speculative frenzy, the chunky hyacinth bulbs, even though spring seems so far away.

Sunny afternoons in late September, fair-weather clouds no longer drift across the sky; now massive, solid, they march down in lockstep from the territory of the northwest passage, heavy with the glint of hidden glaciers and frozen bays.

The cricket and katydid concerts, those pulsating songs of summer days and tangled growth, sound through the lengthening evenings of September and Indian summer and into the fall, until the night you hear only the wind in the dying leaves and realize, as you pull up another blanket, that the insects' summer prophecy, "Six weeks till frost, six weeks till frost," has once again come true.

## II

IN THOSE DAYS before the advent of noisy leaf blowers, every Saturday afternoon from the end of September until Thanksgiving my sister and I were drafted to rake leaves. There were always volunteers that first sunny Saturday the raking season began, when going to battle the leaves seemed a glorious adventure, but the glamour faded quickly, very quickly, and after that the troops could be raised only by conscription.

Our father would lead us, starting along the stone wall below the terrace, teasing the leaves out from among the withering fern fronds, then clearing a foot or two of grass along that front, from the wildflower garden all the way across the lawn to the spring garden. My sister and I followed behind, armed with the large light bamboo rake, whose form fascinated me, and the old maple-handled rake with the blue prongs (who got which depended on the outcome of our argument as to whose turn it was), one after the other raking the brown oak leaves another foot down the yard. This was the easy part, the satisfying part, regaining our lawn, vanquishing the enemy, feeling a sense of accomplishment as the battle waged on and the lawn, foot by foot, was liberated. But when the leaves lay thick or, worse, sodden from a week of rain, every inch of our advance was hard-fought, and our maneuvers had to be interrupted time and again to consolidate our position lest, like Hitler's Russian front, it become unmanageable. Our father laid the old canvas tarp on the lawn right below our line of leaves. Then we'd work from either end, raking and pulling and pushing leaves onto the tarp, rounding up the stragglers and those that tried to elude us. When it was as full as we could manage, we'd pull the four corners of the tarp in toward the center, our father would grab them up in one hand and, like an autumnal Santa Claus, hoist the bulging sack across his back and haul it to the back corner of the yard, where he'd shake out the leaves to begin our pile. Then it was back to neaten up the ragged edges of the line and resume fighting back the enemy, which, since the weekend past, had overrun our yard.

There came a time, always, usually earlier rather than later, when the troops became restless; when the actual possibility of moving the front all the way down the yard to the back garden seemed as costly and improbable as taking Stalingrad; when the tender flap of skin between thumb and trigger finger was beginning to redden and get sore, which presaged the blister that would form by Sunday and split open at school by midweek, exposing new pink skin; when the sky was gray, heavy with war clouds, and the wind pushed the cold around our noses and necks; when tough stems of oak leaves and broken bits of acorns got into our shoes and jabbed our feet, and our shoulders ached, and arguments flared as to who was doing more or who wasn't raking right or who missed some leaves or had those leaves fallen since that area was raked or whose turn was it to use which rake, because the bamboo rake was too light for the matted layer of wet leaves, and clumps of oak leaves kept getting stuck between the blue prongs of the old maple-handled rake and had to be pulled out after every few strokes, and how many millions of leaves there were on a big tree. But throughout the arguments that flared and subsided continued the regular rhythmic swish of our father's rake and the more erratic heave and drag of ours, so that by the time the cold sun was squeezed below the clouds behind the Zeiglers' trees, the line of battle had reached the back of our yard and the pile of leaves was taller than us.

Wise is the commander who lets his troops do a bit of senseless pillaging after battle. My sister and I would take a running start and belly-flop onto that irresistible pile of autumn, millions of brown oak leaves, leathery like mummi-fied tree hands; the soft-as-suede, sweet-smelling maple leaves that looked, in shape and color, exactly like an autumn leaf should; the tulip-tree leaves that had drifted over from the Picketts' yard; the dogwood leaves, crisp and crinkly and easy to rake up from beneath those friendly trees; yellow crab-apple leaves and birch leaves, so tiny and light they hardly counted, all mixed together in one enormous pile that cushioned our increasingly reckless dives.

When the pile began drifting, the leaves escaping back onto the lawn where they wanted to be, our leave was over and the pile had to be manhandled back into shape. Then the fun began. We'd crumple pages of newspaper and stick them deep in all around, our father would strike a match and light these torches, one after another, the paper would catch and blacken and flare, then a leaf or two would singe and we'd watch and watch until at once the pile from deep within would ignite with a terrifying roar, flames leaping wildly, smoke puffing high into the dusky sky like Indian smoke signals. These signals would be sure to catch our mother's attention. Out she'd come to make sure we really knew what we were doing, that we were not about to burn down the Picketts' garage or toast a member of her family. See, we have the hose all ready, we'd show her, like the Smokey Bear fire deputies we were, the lengths of green garden hose snaking from the faucet on the side of the house all the way down the yard to within shooting distance of the bonfire.

As we stood and watched, the leaves waiting in the trees cackled in the wind, laughing, taunting us with the certainty that by the time we got home from school on Monday, reinforcements would have arrived, the lawn would again be theirs, our victory Pyrrhic indeed. We didn't care; we'd won this battle. The war could wait.

Some of those chilly evenings, when the smoke swam up toward the purple clouds, the bonfire seemed a witch's cauldron. Other times, watching the fire stirred images of a Civil War battlefield, of Julia Ward Howe's "watch-fires of a hundred circling camps," a hymn that must have been written in autumn, with its haunting line of "trampling out the vintage where the grapes of wrath are stored." Or we were George Washington's sentinels during the Revolution, stationed a mile down the road on Beacon Hill, scanning the lowlands for signs of British invasion, and when we saw those damn redcoats, our log pyramid stuffed with dried leaves and twigs and topped with a thirty-foot sapling—one of a chain of twenty-three beacons around New Jersey, from Trenton to Princeton to Jockey Hollow to Sandy Hook—would be torched to spread the alarm: "They're coming! They're coming!"

Today, of course, a squadron of landscapers armed with cyclonic leaf blowers, and smaller units strapped to their backs like grenade launchers, can finish in a half hour with time to spare, the job it would take a father and his two young children all afternoon to complete. Today the burning of leaves has been banned; leaves have become a crop to be harvested, shredded, and composted. But even now, a waft of a faraway leaf fire can, like a taste of Proust's dry toast dipped in tea, bring back those fall evenings as we stood by the bonfire keeping warm, or busied ourselves with raking up the straying leaves, when there was something satisfying, something serene, something seasonal about a job well done, the flickering flames, the glowing embers around the base, the crinkle and rustle of leaves being consumed, the crackles and pops of the fire, the jolt as a section of the pile shifted, the autumn smell of raked grass, of smoldering leaves and ashes, and the smoke of the bonfire rising into the coming night.

## III

WE WERE ALWAYS INVOLVED with leaves then. For Miss Hicks, our young second-grade teacher, we'd gladly press leaves under a stack of books over the weekend and bring them in on Monday. Down she'd lead us to the basement art room, where we'd arrange them on pieces of heavy construction paper laid on newspapers spread over the linoleum floor, gleefully—our instincts for making a mess teacher-sanctioned—dipping old toothbrushes into the glass jar of thick red paint, flock-flicking the bristles so the paint would splatter all around the leaf, waiting restlessly, as Miss Hicks read to us in her soothing singsong voice, for the paint to dry at least partially, and then slowly, carefully, lifting each leaf by its stem to reveal its image outlined by the splatters of paint. Another fall, for Mrs. McClellan, we'd bring our harvest of leaves into the kitchen after supper, laying them between squares of waxed paper set out down the ironing board, watching as our mother ran the warm iron over the waxed paper, sealing the leaves inside like insects in amber. For Mrs. Geckler, our seventh-grade science teacher, we mounted leaves on stiff paper and then printed under each the name we found in the *Golden Nature Guide to Trees,* trying to distinguish the similar ones, excited when we found one we couldn't identify, sure we'd discovered in our neighborhood a species new to science.

Blessed are those teachers who give such enduring assignments, which result in a family outing to the reservation to wander through autumn woods and see the leaves, or a search for seed pods to be mounted in a box (the fat acorns we'd always collected for fun, rose hips from around the front-door trellis, horse chestnuts only Tim knew where to find, so shiny they looked varnished, the scarlet fruit of the dogwood and barberry, pinecones of all sizes, shriveled crab apples), or a collection of dried wildflowers to be spray-painted gold or silver and set in plaster of paris for Thanksgiving centerpieces. Rachel Carson was right, of course, that a child "will never forget the experience of a specially planned early rising and going out in the predawn darkness" to hear, for instance, the dawn chorus of birds in spring, or to hunt at night with a flashlight and identify the chirps and trills of an autumn insect orchestra. Such adventures flame a child's inborn sense of awe and wonder. I remember still the thrill-of-adventure feel, going on a bird watch at Martha's Vineyard when I was eight or nine, of watching a neighbor split open a rock to reveal a fossil.

Carson's point was not that we had to identify the leaves or learn to recognize which constellation was which or build up our life list of birds; it was more basic, more fundamental, that we feel something about our world, not necessarily for inspirational or instructional purposes but rather to have always, at least somewhere in the back of our minds, a sense of wonder about life. As Henry Beston wrote in *The Outermost House*, "The world today is sick to its thin blood for lack of elemental things, for fire before the hands, for water welling from the earth, for air, for the dear earth itself underfoot. . . . The gifts of life are the earth's and they are given to all, and they are the songs of birds at daybreak, Orion and the Bear, and dawn seen over ocean from the beach." What assignments were ever more important, what lessons more lasting, than the ones like collecting leaves? The gift Rachel Carson wished for everyone was "a sense of wonder so indestructible that it would last throughout life. . . . Those who dwell, as scientists or laymen, among the beauties and mysteries of the earth are never alone or weary of life. Whatever the vexations or concerns of their personal lives, their thoughts can find paths that lead to inner contentment and to renewed excitement in living. Those who contemplate the beauty of the earth find reserves of strength that will endure as long as life lasts." This must be what Thoreau felt when he said, "There can be no very black melancholy to him who lives in the midst of Nature and has his senses still. . . . While I enjoy the friendship of the seasons I trust that nothing can make life a burden to me."

Fall's spectacle of leaves, this extravaganza, is produced each year for a three-month run, another opening, another show, each day a new cast, new songs and dances, new scenery; yet most of us, most of the time, don't even know it's playing. We don't see the ads, we don't read the reviews, we don't hear the buzz. If it were advertised from September through November, what words, what superlatives, what exclamations, what endorsements, how many thumbs-up would it take to grab our attention? "It's extraordinary how we go through life with eyes half shut, with dull ears, with dormant thoughts," wrote Joseph Conrad in *Lord Jim.* "Perhaps it's just as well," he added; "and it may be that it is this very dullness that makes life to the incalculable majority so supportable and so welcome. Nevertheless, there can be but few of us who had never known one of those rare moments of awakening when we see, hear, understand ever so much—everything—in a flash—before we fall back again into our agreeable somnolence." What does it take to pierce our self-absorption, to trigger one of those fleeting moments of consciousness, of sight, when we see the extraordinary, when life is enchantment? What would open our eyes? Not being able to see something for a while? "Oh beautiful world! Oh beautiful world!" Oscar Wilde exclaimed upon observing a bush in bloom on the day of his release from the Reading prison. Knowing we will never see it again? "Oh, earth," Emily cried out at the end of Thornton Wilder's *Our Town,* looking back at Grover's Corners, "you're too wonderful for anybody to realize you!" Because we know we can see it every day, any day, we tend not to see it at all.

A specially planned trip isn't necessary: it's all right here. Sunlight through leaves goldens the road while I walk down to Memorial Field. Leaves, the exact red-yellow I crayoned for Miss Hicks, flutter and swirl in eddies along the side of the road when a car drives by, and crack and crunch and levitate as I kick through them. On the corner, the maple tree is colored so perfectly it wouldn't be believed if it were painted; green leaves at the base shading up to a layer of yellow and, at the top, the proverbial red flame. Out beyond the softball diamond, the old sugar maple that has known a hundred or more autumns is dropping its leaves one by one onto the grass, into the pool of molten gold around it, leaves that, if their color could be preserved, would have been cast before some ancient Asian potentate. Over by the swings and jungle gym are trees that look like they modeled for a spooky Halloween card.

On such an afternoon in October, you can sit down on the bench by the swings, lean back, gaze up, and watch the show. It's time for the fall, and in a breeze barely perceptible, the marmalade leaves let go one after the other, some drifting down like weekend parachutists, others coming down in a gust with grim determination, like a division of paratroopers dropped behind enemy lines, others descending in style, riding the air currents like surfers cutting back and forth across the face of a wave, others with a final flourish that bores a hole through the blue as if they are figure skaters executing a triple axle. Some ride down joyfully, others shyly, others as timidly as seventh-graders climbing down the rope from the ceiling of the gym.

A leaf swirls down from the old oak by the tennis courts, catching in the birch branches below, clinging on for dear life, holding fast, halfway to earth. Come on, leaf, it's not so bad down here. No, it's not what you're used to, up where you've been all spring and summer like some green god in that blue sky, greeting each sunrise. It's the trip down, that's what you fear, isn't it? And what comes next, once you're down away from where you should be. Hey, there'll be a soft landing, I promise; and before you know it, you'll be a part of a tree again. And the breeze blows and the leaf lets go and twirls, slowly, to the grass.

A few weeks later, the big leaves of the ash at the top of the driveway have colored, and even on this drizzly fall afternoon, its dazzling yellow lights up the area outside my window as if the day were sunny, the leaves are that electric. When the sky is October blue, the tree seems lit by spotlights. I took a photograph of it once on a perfect fall day, looking straight up through the leaves with the blue sky between, focusing on the two colors, the yellow of the leaves and the blue October sky, to determine if my eyes could be registering those colors accurately, or were somehow tricked by the splendor of the scene. The snapshot recorded the yellow and blue just as I was seeing them, two colors that glow from the photograph even when I look at it on a winter's day. That smaller ash growing in the front bank, it seeded itself years ago when no one was looking and is positioned out of symmetry. So each summer, when its big leaves are green and tough, I stare and stare at it and consider cutting it down. It would be a simple matter; the trunk of the tree is only inches in diameter, and it would fall perfectly across the road, where I could easily drag it and topple it down over the ridge. But then I remember how those leaves will glow in the fall, and asymmetry or not, cutting it down is out of the question.

Daily, fall's palette of oil paints mixes and mingles, and the leaves left in the trees after a wild night of wind and rain are the dusky colors of smeared-on war paint, browns mixed in with dark reds and golds. Maybe Indians did, as legend has it, bury a chief killed in battle beneath a partially uprooted young tree, carefully laying the body there in the root hollow dressed in full chieftain regalia, then straightening the tree, which, over the years, would grow above, reflecting his glory in the autumn when it put on its colors. It's hard to imagine a finer monument than a tree (better by far than a granite marker in a creepy cemetery), a tree in all seasons, growing up toward the sun, the breezes blowing through its leaves, hosting birds and squirrels in its boughs, nourishing the soil with its fallen leaves. In time, the chieftain's body would find its way into the being of the tree, into the soul of its miracles. "Lay my ashes at the foot of a dogwood tree," wrote Irvin S. Cobb; "should the tree live, that will be monument enough for me."

# IV

A BUMPER CROP of acorns covers the lawn, so many you could skate across the grass as if on ball bearings, and the squirrels are dancing, dazed with the bounty. Never go to the supermarket when you're hungry, my mother advised me when I set out on my own, advice squirrel mothers should give their children. For every hole they dig to bury an acorn when they look around and think no one's watching, they sit back on their haunches and, like late-night TV addicts with the munchies, devour two more. The squirrels deposit their acorns, the chipmunk who has begged for salted mixed cocktail nuts all summer long—gobbling a few but always racing home with the biggest—must by now have filled his burrow to the rafters, the bees are guzzling pollen, all wisely augmenting their IRA accounts, saving for a rainy day, for the long winter ahead. For a month, birds have been feasting on the tiny crab apples hanging from the bare tree outside my front door. The mourning doves arrive first in the morning, then families of robins, then the late risers, the blue jays, who bully away the others, except the squirrels dropping by all day to sample the orange fruit at this drive-through McDonald's window, and still, at the end of each day, there seem to be just as many left.

No matter what the garden catalogs breathlessly promise

about perennials blooming from June to first frost, they have by now thrown in the towel, all except the last brave flowers of autumn. These are the most beautiful, the ones that appear against all odds after weeks of frosty mornings and soaking rains that bring down most of the leaves. There, on one of those unexpected dividend days of Indian summer, there, poking through the oak leaves, the yellow flower of a Stella de Oro daylily, one, just one, above the withered stalks and seed pods from the summer's abundance, tiny, smaller than June's but more exquisite in its waxy, orchidlike, solitary perfection, waiting patiently, hopefully, for a sluggish bee making its final rounds in the remaining warmth of high noon. The last Shasta daisy blooming after all the others have given up, the last rose, the final coreopsis, going on, doing its thing against insuperable odds. They're like Mrs. Dubose in Harper Lee's *To Kill a Mockingbird*, the old lady who was determined to break her morphine addiction before she died. That's real courage, Atticus explained to Jem and Scout, "when you know you're licked before you begin but you begin anyway and you see it through no matter what." These last flowers of autumn, the courageous ones, are the most beautiful.

The unexpected appear now, too. White begonias, distant descendants of ones planted in that bed before I turned it into the perennial garden, have seeded themselves, survived repeated scorched-earth weedings, and bloom happily among the fallen black-eyed Susans. Here we are, they proclaim, right where you wanted us! The white and purple impatiens, great-grandchildren of ones bought years ago at the nursery, are also back, under the shelter of hosta leaves where their seeds scattered and took hold, one with an incredibly colored flower, a cross-pollination of purple and white blended to a striking new mauve, a color for Alexandra's boudoir in the Winter Palace. Other seeds lodged between the bricks of the walks, survived two annual applications of bleach to remove the slippery moss from the bricks, hid from the vegetation killer—Agent Orange in an aerosol can—sprayed wherever a suspicious touch of green appeared along the paths, took root in that inhospitable bed of crushed stone and quarry dust beneath the brick and now, at the tail end of the season, in an extraordinary burst of will, shoot up between the bricks to proudly display their one tiny yet perfect flower atop their stunted stems. Here, surely, was Tennyson's flower in the crannied wall: "If I could understand / What you are, root and all, and all in all, / I should know what God and man is." To understand these courageous impatiens that don't give up, that keep trying even in the most unlikely places and under the most discouraging circumstances, may well be to understand everything.

The flowers of these late bloomers are as remarkable as the stories of life's late bloomers, people like Anna Mary Robertson, better known as Grandma Moses, a hired girl and later a wife of a farmer in New York, who began painting at the age of seventy-six when arthritis made her give up her embroidery. Her canvases were not appreciated as extraordinary works until she was into her eighties. Or how about those whose work, for one reason or another, isn't recognized until years and years after it should have been, people like Helen Hooven Santmyer, who, in her thirties, wrote a novel, . . . *And Ladies of the Club,* which did not find a publisher until half a century later when, at eighty-eight, blind in one eye with a cataract in the other, her eighty-pound body wracked by emphysema and confined to her wheelchair in her book-filled room at Hospitality Home East, a nursing home in her hometown of Xenia, Ohio, she saw her book published to become a best-seller and front-page media event.

To those who didn't make life's first cut, or second, or third, who weren't genetically endowed to become high school's peppy cheerleaders or homecoming queens or football captains, who weren't accepted at the colleges of their choice or hired for the jobs they coveted or granted the acceptance or recognition they deserved, who would never be the awe-inspiring blooms of May and June that elicit all the raves, who went through a lifetime of no one noticing but yet plugged on, who played out with pluck and flair the tough hand life dealt them, who kept trying, who didn't give up: surely these late bloomers are the most beautiful of them all.

A dreamy day of Indian summer, the air soft and warm in the sunlight beyond the shadows, sweet with the smell of dying leaves. In the shady far corner of the terrace garden, in the pool nestled among ferns and outcroppings, the lazy goldfish glide through the green-dark water, back and forth as they have for years, materializing like phantom deer, glimpses of orange scattering under the trickle of water splashing down the rocks into the pool, suspended for a moment in water, regrouping for yet another tour of their kingdom, then disappearing into the depths.

Like a visitor, I wander the brick paths through the back gardens to see what's left. In May the garden without drifts of Virginia bluebells punctuated by clumps of red tulips, without the daffodils and hyacinths and the backdrop of forsythia and the fragrance of the lilacs, is unthinkable. In early summer, we wish the perennial garden would continue on just as it is till frost. But on reflection, who would want it all at once? Tulips and chrysanthemums all season long would be as jarring, as unnatural, as the new trend of featuring pansies in the fall. Gardens are like those extraordinary Fabergé eggs made for the czars, revealing surprise after surprise as the season progresses, each week showing some new wonder. Can there be any doubt that the priest of Ecclesiastes who knew that "for everything there is a season" was a gardener? Gardeners never have a chance to look back or worry about today; they're too busy waiting for tomorrow.

Looking at lichens on a stone wall wouldn't cut it in the spring, but isn't it funny how it seems just right, right now? I stare at them as if at peonies. "Late in life I have come on fern," wrote Robert Frost in his poem "Leaves Compared with Flowers"; "Now lichens are due to have their turn." Everything to its age, everything to its season. Now I look not at flowers but at the individual stones in the wall that had been hidden by the withered brown and fallen perennials, and spot the robin's nest in the crux of the viburnum, ah, so that's where it was, and the squirrel's nest high in the oak in the back of the yard and the messy crow's nest in the treetops across the road, and notice the bright red berries of the prickly barberries and the hollies and the clusters of orange-red firethorn berries, and collect some of the tiny cones that pull so easily from the branches of the spruce and save them in a mason jar, and run my fingers through the soft silver foliage of the dianthus, and stare, amazed, at the architecture of the trees.

Up in the birch two crows sit together on a branch.

Crows like to think they're thugs, tough guys, badgering other birds, their raucous debates and arguments awakening the neighborhood, gangs of them forming and swooping as though ready for a rumble. The two sitting side by side, high on the birch branch bouncing in the breeze, would have been embarrassed if they knew I was watching. One began preening the other, gently, very gently, picking at the smooth, tiny black feathers on top of its head, pulling, arranging, rearranging the head feathers like the most artistic hairstylist, the other crow really grooving on this, leaning closer, nestling its head against the hairstylist's chest in total contentment as they rode on the branch in the autumn breeze.

## V

STOPPING ON THE WAY HOME at the roadside nursery to buy a Halloween pumpkin is like walking into an Edward Hopper painting: the cold slant of autumn light at the end of the day; the piles of pumpkins and sheaves of cornstalks and bales of hay around the shed; the grin of a jack-o' lantern by the cash register; the attendants in plaid wool jackets and gloves, waiting to close up, dancing in place to keep warm; the smell of bushel baskets of apples and gallon jugs of cider and homemade doughnuts and pumpkin pies; the darkness beyond the shed.

It's dark when I pay and put the pumpkin and cider in the car. There are no evenings darker than the first days after the end of daylight saving time, when the clocks are set back and suddenly, unexpectedly, it's night at five o'clock when it should still be light, the earth turning away from the sun, spinning farther out into those vast, lonely reaches of space, the days shortening, shortening. Dark and cold. The wind pushes the cold through my jacket and around my neck. Get out an extra blanket tonight. And better check the furnace.

Dry leaves scuffle across the parking lot in the wind. Skeletal branches of bare trees claw at the twilight sky like the bony arms and grasping fingers of a witch. Charcoal and violet clouds scud and swirl across the moon.

I hurry home, glad to reach my street, the houses indistinguishable from the night shadows and trees except for squares of curtained light, behind which there will be the smells of cooking, and maybe talking, someone practicing the piano, the pages of a newspaper turning.

With the night comes the wind, and with the wind the cold, and by morning winter is in the air.

## VI

ALL DAY heavy clouds gather, massing until they blanket the sky, bringing darkness an hour before nightfall, and with the dark come heavy rains, shrapnel of sleet at the windows and roof, ice on the trees. "Implacable November weather," as Dickens described such a day in *Bleak House*—this too-early taste of the sun's retreat, of shorter days to come, of the long winter ahead—the kind of day Melville wrote about in *Moby-Dick,* that puts "a damp, drizzly November" in the soul, that made Ishmael pause before coffin warehouses and bring up the rear of every funeral procession encountered.

The sullen rains continue until Saturday, a blowy, sunny day when the ice loosens from the bare branches overhead, and ice crystal crashes onto the roof all morning. The water in the birdbath where the junco dunked and splashed just a few days ago is frozen. Leaves lie packed in the gutters, and the marigolds, the begonias, the ageratum in the sunny front beds have disappeared. "Disappeared" seems exactly the right word for their vanishing, one day blooming as always, as if they intend to stay around all winter, the next day not even recognizable, all color gone, the begonias a pulpy mash, the ageratum nothing but a tangle of woody twigs, the marigolds stripped of their lemon-drop splendor. The white and purple impatiens along the back border look somewhat bedraggled; their white flowers still shine, but that's a brave front. When they unfreeze in the sun, they wilt instantly, their watery stems collapsing, the flowers that lit the border all spring and summer and fall nowhere to be found. One or two of the late bloomers are still trying, bravely carrying on as if nothing has happened, the ones huddled in the pachysandra, shivering, a blanket of oak leaves pulled up to their chins. They will keep going as long as they can.

At the end of the season, when it's time to write up performance reports and decide which players will be on the team next year, I never cut annuals from my list. Trendy gardeners may raise their eyebrows and sniff as if annuals' appearance in anything other than wooden tubs around gasoline stations is an unpardonable breach of gardening etiquette (how is it that service-station annuals always look so good? Is it the full sun or something about those delicious gasoline fumes?), but the reality is that these players perform. They don't need coddling and don't ask for signing bonuses.

Four flats of marigolds, two flats of ageratum, four flats of begonias massed in the small boxwood-bordered beds out front around the goldfish pond, blooming nonstop from the day of their arrival to the day of their disappearance. Sure, some marigold flowers have to be snapped off every day or two to keep them blooming well, and every once in a while there's that sticky mucus trail leading straight to the heart of the bed that requires yet another application of slug poison, but that's a small price for seven, maybe eight months of Mary's gold, the Virgin Mary's flower that decorated medieval churches. The ageratum, a real blue, and the begonias, a real white, bloom on and on, on their own, without fuss or bother.

And the impatiens! From that first sunny Saturday morning in April when my neighbor sees me in the backyard on my hands and knees, squeezing the miniature impatiens, each with a tiny white or purple flower, out of the plastic containers and tucking them in all along the border, and calls over, "You're brave!" (what she really means is "You're crazy!" as it's several weeks before the last possible frost date, and that's a lot of work to repeat if six flats of impatiens are wiped out, but the year's at the spring and day's at the morn, it's a sunny Saturday, and I can't bear to wait any longer), from then until the first killing frost, on the impatiens go. The border where I plant them is under the hollies and pines, the soil so rocky and root-bound I can barely scrape away enough soil to tuck them in, let alone dig them decent holes. They don't care, that's fine for them. There's no need to deadhead them, fertilize them, stake them; they aren't afraid of slugs or rabbits, groundhogs or deer, for that matter; they don't mind the sun, they don't mind the shade; they're immune to mildew and mold; they don't get leggy or need to be trimmed back. They're anxious to play all season, not just for several games, like most of the perennials, which then want to go inside and sit in front of the television, drinking beer and hoping to do an occasional endorsement or to win the perennial-of-the-year award. Come November's frost when the show is over, they just disappear. They don't need to be cut down or dug up or hauled away. Poof, like that they're gone, and as a dividend, they leave behind their seeds, which add to next year's bounty. Throughout the season, as long as the underground water sprinkler hits them once or twice a week (they're not like some of the more persnickety plants that can't stand to get their leaves wet or need their roots soaked or have other nonnegotiable demands), they do exactly what they're supposed to do. On those steamy days that start late in July, when it hasn't rained for weeks and everything else in the garden has taken one look around and decided to stop growing, when black-eyed Susans look fatigued and the daisies begin to swoon, when hosta flowers are fading and it's slipped the minds of the Stella de Oros that they're supposed to be ever-blooming, when even the old forsythia has stopped sending out new growth and its leaves are drooping, the impatiens never look better. These natives of Zanzibar, brought to Europe in

1865, feel right at home in a sweltering suburban Guadal-canal, and their blossoms seem daily to get bigger and brighter. Day after day. That is what's amazing. Not only through the humid days of August, but each day bigger, brighter, into the cooler days of September and October, lighting up the border, as dependable as Eagle Scouts. Is it any wonder that there are more impatiens sold in the United States than all other annuals combined?

If Luther Burbank were alive today, he would be trying to cross just such an annual with a perennial. What we need are plants with all these Eagle Scout qualities that also will rise again each year or, alternatively, perennials with the sexual stamina of annuals. Why can't an annual, as every gardener wonders and as Henry Higgins would have sung it, be more like a perennial? Hybriders have fiddled with the sex lives of perennials to try to prolong the relatively short period in which they flower and produce seed, but this work has not come even close to replicating the orgies of annuals, which do it again and again and again with gusto, all season long ("Busy Lizzie," the English call impatiens). You can tell, for instance, when the Stella de Oros are really into it in June, as compared to August, when they show about the same enthu-siasm as a middle-aged couple who's done it exactly the same way for the last twenty-three years, to late September, when they're plain old faking it.

# VII

THERE ARE WARM SUNNY DAYS LATER, days when the chrysanthemums continue their show as if they were never enshrouded in ice, days when the annuals would still be blooming had it not been for that one killing frost, days when gardeners are out once again on their knees, worshiping, affirming their unshakable faith by planting spring bulbs, just like E. B. White's wife, Katherine, in her final years "on this awesome occasion—the small, hunched-over figure, her studied absorption in the implausible notion that there would be yet another spring, oblivious to the ending of her own days, which she knew perfectly well was near at hand, sitting there with her detailed chart under those dark skies in the dying October, calmly plotting the resurrection."

But a day comes at last—maybe it's that feel of winter in the air, maybe the smell of it, maybe it has something to do with the pale wintry light, Paul Simon's "hazy shade of winter," something instinctual that suddenly sets the congregations of birds stirring—whatever it is, at last the day comes when you know it's time to batten down for winter.

Orion the Hunter has moved south in the night sky. Earthworms have burrowed deeper. All season long, birds have seemed to live solitary lives, flying alone, feeding alone, but now six, seven, eight robins appear together at the birdbath out back and around the goldfish pool in front, acting as if they're about to start a triathlon: pacing, sipping water, stretching their wings, looking down at their claws, restless to begin. Great flocks of starlings gather in the oak out front, a racket of restless, questioning clicks and clacks and clatter. They swoop to the ground as one, nervously poke among the leaves, then take off as a group, to the tulip tree next door, leapfrogging tree to tree through the neighborhood, and are gone. The temperature has dipped into the twenties and has not risen out of the thirties during the day. There are freak snowstorms out in Cleveland that dumped eleven inches, and snow squalls in upstate New York. For the first time it feels cold, a raw, penetrating-all-the-way-through cold.

"Well, it's that time of year again," Jimmy says, sounding not at all happy as he gets out of his pickup truck early on a dismal November morning. He's come to shut down the sprinkler system.

"Boy, that went fast, didn't it? It seems like you were just here to turn it on."

"Faster each year. At least it seems that way."

He goes to work quickly, professionally, draining the water left in the system, checking each of the stations around the lawn and in the gardens, mothballing the control panel in the furnace room.

"What do you do off-season?" I ask as he climbs back into his truck.

"You know, a little of this, a little of that." He grins, shrugging. "I'll keep busy. Always do, one way or the other. See you next spring!"

"It'll be here before you know it."

"I sure hope so."

The storm windows are in place. All the bulbs have been planted. The soil around the new Norway spruce has been soaked with the hose for half a day. The outside water is turned off, the stiff garden hose drained and, in a scene resembling Laocoön fighting the serpents, manhandled into some semblance of coils and deposited out of the way in the garage. The air-conditioning unit is covered with a tarp, the birdbath turned over, the watering can brought in, the big green bottle that sat next to the perennial garden emptied and stored way back in the corner of the garage where it won't get hit. The burlap windbreaks are up around the boxwood. The gutters have been cleared of their packed overflow of leaves and twigs and acorns, the lawn and gardens swept clean. The perennials have been cut close to the ground, the annuals pulled up and thrown away, the trowels and shovels and rakes and clippers cleaned and in order for spring.

The closing down, the gathering in. Joseph Lincoln, a

popular novelist in the early part of the twentieth century who wrote books set on Cape Cod, told how old New England houses were banked up for winter, how cartloads of dried seaweed were hauled from the beach, pitchforked around the foundations, and pounded down as protection against the howling winter winds; but not even this insulation could keep out the cold: "Often and often we have watched the ingrain carpet in our dining-room lift and lift against its tacked edges and puff up in the middle like a tightly stretched sail, as the blasts seeped through the seaweed barrier and whistled under the beams and boards." *The Old Farmer's Almanac* predicts an unusually hard winter, but all is safely gathered in. Let the winter storms, if they must, begin.

The evening, dark and cold. As I drive home, I'm thinking of the goldfish. Their pool won't ice up without several days of freezing temperatures, and even then, it's deep enough so only the top will freeze over. But I think of them in there, used to their balmy summer swims and the sweet days of Indian summer, when leaves from the tulip tree and birch settled lazily on the surface and they swam around and under with dramatic turns that displayed to best advantage their diaphanous tails. I think of them now on this coming-of-winter evening with the long cold night ahead. When I get home, I dig the pool's heater out from under the workbench and walk back to the garden in the dark, hauling out from the pool the recirculating pump, coated with algae and slime. I turn it over to let the water drain and place the heater in the pool and plug it in. There, for the winter months, it will float on the surface and, when the temperature of the pool drops below freezing, turn on to keep the water open.

What do these goldfish and frogs—all born and orphaned in April and left with no adult supervision—think of the coming of winter? Why would they have any reason to believe the differences they sense are anything other than aberrations, freak days that happen to be colder and darker than the moderate weather they've come to accept as the norm? Or is the change in light and fall in temperature so subtle, so gradual, a minute or two less of brightness each morning and evening, a degree or two cooler every few days, that they adapt to the change as it occurs and don't give it another thought? The goldfish are good sports about it; on any sunny day they'll venture up to the surface to explore, returning to the depths when the low sun slides westward. The frogs, on the other hand, have no intention of sticking around to see if they'll find winter to their liking; before the first frost, they plunge to the bottom of the pool and burrow under a blanket of muck to snooze.

I once had occasion to awaken a frog after its winter nap

had commenced. I had assumed that the raccoons in August ate up every last goldfish in the back pool. Every once in a while I'd sprinkle in a little food, but no fish ever rose from the murky depths to eat, and the next day the food would still be lying on the surface. Over the next months, I never saw any activity whenever I walked by, no flash of gold, no ripple in the water.

Until a warm day in early December when, like Robert Frost cleaning his pasture spring, I stopped to rake the leaves away and spotted a telltale flash of goldfish gold. This guy, I knew, should spend the winter in the front pool, where he'd have some friends, rather than being all alone here in the cold and dark. Shooting fish in a barrel isn't as easy as the expression would imply. With the fish net I dragged the pond looking for him, back and forth, scooping out load after load of rotting leaves, which I dropped into the garden cart, making sure there was nothing moving in the stinking pile. Load after load, back and forth, into the nooks and crannies of the pool, and then there he was, caught in my net. I emptied him into the pail of water I had waiting. As the water in the pool cleared, flash!, another goldfish, which I spent many more minutes chasing through the pond. I kept dredging for good measure, to make sure I hadn't missed a cousin and to clean out the pool as long as I was already mud-splashed, sweaty, and almost finished, pulling out the season's debris as well as the rocks the raccoons had delighted in toppling in. In one pile of wet leaves, a little slimy movement caught my eye: a frog, as groggy with sleep as a child woken before dawn for a trip. Too out of it to let out his "Eek!" and jump four feet as he would have in the summer, he stretched a leg or two and looked around to determine if this was a scene in a froggy winter's dream or some other sort of rude inconvenience. While he debated this, I plopped him into the pail and then brought them all, a frog and two goldfish, to their winter resort in front of the house and dropped them into the pool. They instantly disappeared. All the goldfish in due course surfaced to reacquaint themselves with their long-lost cousins. The frog found it quieter at the bottom of the pool and resumed his sleep to wait out the long night of winter ahead.

# VIII

PURVEYORS OF PLANT PORNOGRAPHY are more sinister, more sophisticated, more insidious than the raunchiest merchants of old Forty-second Street. They print their lurid catalogs months in advance and address them to those whose names have been culled from mailing lists of individuals known to be pitifully weak and susceptible to temptation.

Then, like loathsome predators, they lie in wait, monitoring the long-range weather forecasts for the right day to flash their wares.

We know from experience exactly what day it will be, though because of our proclivities, we never are able to marshal our defenses to "just say no." It will be, invariably, inevitably, a winter's day, not any winter's day but specifically Robert Frost's "darkest evening of the year" day, a dreary day of overcast gloom and cold gray drizzle. By late afternoon it's already so dark out it could be night. And that's when you hear it. You look up from your desk, startled, and listen. No, it can't be: that insistent tinkling on your cold windowpane sounds like sleet.

You turn out the lights in your office and close the door so you can see outside. It's not a pretty sight. In the pale penumbra of the parking lot's cold fluorescent lights, fellow workers are leaving the building, cautiously walking over shiny blacktop. Already the grass around the parking lot is whitening. A woman bundled like a Russian peasant in a quilted coat and winter boots teeters, almost slips, rights herself, and then proceeds as if on a balance beam, baby step by baby step, out to her car. Others are turning on their engines, opening their trunks, digging out their scrapers and working on the windshields glazed with ice, their coats buttoned up around their necks, their scarves and hair blowing about, the exhaust from tailpipes whipped into the dark. Scrape, scrape, scrape: you hear that rasping, spine-tingling sound even here, on the third floor, the sound of ice thick enough to skate on being chipped and cracked from glass. The first cars slip and skid as they come to the stop sign at the bottom of the hill, and in the distance, sirens sound. The police and rescue squads will be working overtime tonight.

The commuter's dilemma: leave now, before it gets any worse? Or wait until the rush-hour traffic clears? Like a dutiful Bob Cratchit, you go back to work, but before long, you look outside again. Now it's not just the grass beyond the lot that's white. The ice on the parking lot has been covered over with snow, it's coming down now, and workers are pouring out of the building as if it grazed an iceberg, took on a nasty list, and is about to capsize. Raised eyebrows and scowls of oh-so-dedicated and foolhardy fellow workers notwithstanding, it's every man for himself, the women and children be damned: abandon ship!

Outside, it's even worse than it looked. Your feet feel the ice under the snow, and as you turn the heater on high and leave the dark cocoon of the car to brush off snow and scrape ice as quickly as possible before more accumulates, you devise your game plan. The sanders and plows haven't come by yet; are the roads even passable? You have good tires, a heavy car, a full tank, front-wheel drive. Slow, steady, keep the forward momentum going, and you'll get home when you get home.

It's working. You feel the treachery of the roads but compensate by crawling along in low gear, following in the tracks of the car ahead, not too close so you won't have to stop suddenly, just steady, inch by inch, homeward bound, humming a rendition of Scarlett O'Hara's refrain: "Just a few more miles to tote the weary load." The other commuters must be of like mind, for a slow, orderly procession of cars winds its way along the road through the storm.

And then, out of the swirling snowy mists, appears from nowhere a car ahead of you, you know which one, the same one that, like the abominable snowman, makes its mysterious appearance in every blizzard as commuters struggle home. Yes, it's that one, the big old boat of a car ahead of you, the one you know won't be able to surmount the slight rise in the road no steeper than a stack of five or six paper napkins.

"You can do it, old man," you find yourself saying aloud, though is its driver a man? Maybe. Could it be a woman? Perhaps. All you can see through the thud of your frozen wipers, fighting to keep open a diminishing amount of windshield, is a huge head and some sort of furry coat, which, come to think of it, is the exact description mountaineers have provided of their glimpses of the abominable snowman in the high reaches of the Himalayas.

"Steady, old man, just take it nice and steady, don't stop, as long as you don't stop, you'll be okay, just keep—"

The red brake lights flash on, the car goes into a sickening, erratic skid, stops, and then ("No! No! Please don't do it") the driver guns his engine.

Wheels spin and dig into snow and ice. What to do next? ("No, no, I beg of you, please don't!") Why, step on the gas again, this time harder, longer. The wheels are smoking, the car shudders, trembles, then settles deeper into the ice grave it's digging. What now? Now you only shake your head in silent benediction. You know it's all over as Yeti goes for the big one: floor it! A horrible, storm-rending screech as the car pours on more thrust than would be necessary to get a 747 airborne off an aircraft carrier. But a car is not a 747, and now the worst sound of all: silence. The car's lights flicker out. Did he blow his engine? Has he given up? Did the carbon monoxide from his attempted interplanetary launch do him in? Is he going to sit there and wait out the storm? You look in the rearview mirror and see the glow of a line of cars extending as far down the road as you can see. Of course, someone honks his horn. Yes, that will help. Then, farther down the line, another horn answers, either telling the first horn to knock it off or seconding the motion. Soon, way down the line, others join in; not all together but one then another and another, until a grating, maddening rhythm develops.

There is nothing to be done. Yeti has quite completely blocked the road, his car having come to its final resting place in a peculiarly perpendicular position. The line of cars traveling the opposite direction, in orderly fashion, slowing to do a bit of rubbernecking, make pulling out and around impossible. Yeti is stuck. You are stuck. They are stuck. We all are stuck.

Snow is falling faster. Your wipers fight the good fight, but on each downward sweep, they compress the heavy snow into solid-pack ice that, minute by minute, grows higher up the windshield, cutting visibility. The side windows are covered, and the back window, despite the window heater, offers only a hazy glimpse of the spectral white lights behind you. It's dark inside the car. Against the hiss of snow and sleet and the breathing of the heater, the horns begin to sound faraway, soothing, almost like a lullaby. You settle back in the seat. "The woods are lovely, dark, and deep," your mind hums, "the woods are lovely dark and—" You sit up with a start: carbon-monoxide poisoning? You open the window to let in some fresh air, and soon the two fingers on your left hand that were frostbitten years ago begin to feel rubbery. Can't sit here forever. Got to get out of here. Now! Got to get out! Losing it! The edges of panic have set in, and around those edges new plans begin to take shape. Abandon car on side of road and walk home. Ten miles in a blizzard can be a long way; remember Per Hansa. Gun the engine and ram Yeti off the road. Your car could get damaged, and you don't have time next week to take it to the shop. Very slowly move forward and shove him sideways out of—

Wait! Yeti has climbed out. He is looking around. He huddles back in. His lights flicker on, he guns the engine. Again. And again. The car rocks and rolls and, with a roar and a lurch, breaks free from its ice coffin and moves forward into the snow.

Thank you, thank you, you pray, putting your car in drive, easing forward, feeling the wheels spin on the ice and then catch, rumbling and crunching over the mysterious yeti tracks and then onward. You reinstate your game plan, revising it to follow a maze of back roads and side streets, risking drifts of virgin snow to avoid any more encounters with abominable snowmen.

At last you reach your driveway, though the journey is not yet over; Tara still lies ahead. The driveway goes pretty much straight up, angling along the side of the ridge, and one slip of the wheels over the snow-covered Belgian-block edge and the car will roll down the embankment, flip over on the road, slide down the ridge, landing on its roof far below in the woods, bursting into flames, as in the best action flick. So no power will drain from the engine, you shut down the wipers, the heater, the defroster, the back-window heater, take a running start, and plow up that drive through the ice and snow, the car quivering halfway up, the wheels veering the wrong way, toward the Belgian-block edge, don't stop, don't stop, can't stop or it's all over, straighten, straighten, the wheels spin, on, on, one hand off the wheel, don't stop, press the garage-door opener, the garage-door swings up, keep going, the beckoning light in the garage urges you on, on car, toward that lovely, warm, welcoming orifice, into it, front wheels grasp the dry floor of the garage, you're in, home, you got it, you turn off the engine, unfasten your hands finger by finger from the wheel, and inhale, realizing at last that you've been holding your breath for quite some time. Feeling not unlike Sir Ernest Shackleton after his voyage in an open boat across Antarctica, you stumble out of the car, close the garage door, and go into the house.

It's that kind of night. So when you open the front door and take in the mail, the fact that this is the night the plant predators have earmarked to tempt you is the last thing on your mind. You are thankful to be home out of the storm, thankful that the power hasn't been knocked out by the ice, thankful that the heat is coming up, thankful that the oven is warming and that there are enough leftovers for an easy dinner, thankful that tomorrow is Saturday and you don't have to go out. You hang up your wet coat and scarf and take a quick thumb-through of the mail before you change into something more comfortable. American Express bill, telephone bill, a solicitation from your college fund-raising campaign, a credit-card company's offer to lend $5,000, no questions asked, the bill from the plumber who fixed the leak yesterday, catalogs from Pottery Barn, Hammacher Schlemmer, Charles Keath, out, out, out, and then, placed discreetly underneath the Horchow catalog, there they are: the spring gardening catalogs.

With longing gazes, you stare at those glossy beguiling covers and already feel better, much better. The assurance at the bottom of the covers—"Satisfaction Guaranteed"—hardly seems necessary. You turn the pages, every now and then wiping a little drool from the corner of your mouth, ogling masses of hardy carnations, each as perfect as a boutonniere snatched from a groom's tuxedo: hosta with leaves washed, waxed, and polished to green perfection; bearded iris, whose subtle spring-grape fragrance seems to waft up from the page as if from a perfume advertisement; ferns transplanted from some rain forest where dinosaurs still wander; tulips in wild, wonderful vibrating colors as if hand-painted by van Gogh; dazzling bouquets of peonies as delicious as rainbow sherbet; hyacinths, masses of hyacinths you could bury your face in (careful always, though, with those hyacinths, as it was a hyacinth analogy that landed Oscar Wilde in jail). Page by page you paw through, imagining how each plant will look in your garden and what sort of relationship you will have with it, the close-ups of dewy, creamy, smooth flowers as innocent as a sweet sixteen, others with a graceful, demure, aristocratic bearing promising seasons of luxurious splendor, others boldly flaunting their knockout looks. Which do you like the best? Why, tonight you like them all and will order them all, your own plant harem.

How many times in real life have you seen a model? Have you ever seen a model shopping at the mall? Has one ever sat next to you on a plane? Do you pass them on busy city streets or catch glimpses of them at trendy restaurants? Of course not. And the plant and flower models you see in these catalogs are just as likely to make an appearance in your garden. On such a night—and this is what the plant pornographers know so well—your eyes don't see the makeup, the implants, the dye, the wigs, you're not even vaguely aware of the lifts, the tucks, the liposuction, the collagen implants, the petal augmentation, you don't know that these high-maintenance plants are working out at the gym four nights a week and slurping down Miracle-Gro shakes and injecting steroids. Nor do any of the tricks of lighting and photography disturb your misty thoughts. Such gardens of Eden, which have you so enchanted and entranced, truly exist only in the pages of plant pornography and in the minds of gardeners.

But the promises, all those promises, what of the promises?

The age-old promises are all there in the descriptions beneath the photos, enough to arouse a gardener's prurient interest and awaken springtimes of possibilities—"a continuous parade of luxurious summer color"; "hardy"; "mildew-free"; "strong stems"; "summer-long garden beauty"; "forty-three blossoms on each stem"; "return with renewed vigor each year"—all those wonderful old oxymoronic promises: "perennial tulips," "drought-resistant," "four-season petunias," "shade-tolerant," "continuous bloom," "white marigolds," "blue roses." It's the kind of night when the promise "Yeah, sure, I'll respect you in the morning" sounds like a solemn eternal commitment memorialized in marble; you have no reason to doubt it. You want to believe. If it were any other night, you would remember how long your Stella de Oro lilies really bloom, or don't, each year. But your mind has blanked out the reality of flabby flower thighs and pimply plant backs, and you make a notation to order two dozen more, no, make that three dozen, to fill in that back border with a continuous parade of summer color.

Tonight your warm, fuzzy feelings extend beyond the

flowers and plants to all the sick fantasy devices displayed in these pages. A trowel is a trowel is a trowel, Gertrude Stein may have said, but this is the sort of night when a $58 trowel with a hand-carved mahogany handle and a blade forged in Tuscany seems to make a lot of sense as the tool you've needed to plant properly; a night when a set of three trowels of different sizes for digging holes for different-size plants makes even more sense; a night when French-enamel wheelbarrows and English-copper watering cans strike you as not only practical necessities but sensuous works of art; when you can picture yourself next spring on an Oriental kneeling stool, easing out weeds with your new carbon-steel hand weeder and tossing them into your Egyptian woven weeding basket. It is a night when everything Martha Stewart does suddenly makes eminent sense, and you know that next spring you'll finally have the time to undertake a lot of her projects. In fact, you may well want to press some of your more interesting weeds with a hardwood flower press and preserve them in collages or glue them onto lamp shades.

Seasoned gardeners know from experience not to place their orders on such a stormy night. No, better to spend some quality time with the catalogs tomorrow in the sunroom on the loveseat next to the shelf of Christmas cactus and geranium cuttings, studying the pages as the afternoon sunlight moves below the catalog along your legs and melts across the floor. It's good to be in when it's too cold to be outside and the wind sweeps through the hemlocks and bare branches of the oaks and moves the sunlight on the floor, to savor the catalogs and smell the moist potting soil and the greenness of the geranium leaves next to you and envision your own garden of Eden.

The winter night comes quickly, and soon it's too dark to read. You gather the catalogs and put them away in case anyone stops by. Out the back window, through tops of trees, the small cold sun has already fallen below the tangle of branches, leaving behind colors like narrow bands of frozen ices, orange and lemon and raspberry, a line of blackberry extending farther out, and then the blue and purple and black of night. After dinner you go outside, crunching through the glazed crust of snow, to visualize the best site for a bed of Asiatic lilies. Snow drifts surround the fish pond, but the deicer has kept the water open, and beneath the surface the goldfish doze around the heating element. The night wind pummels the cold through trousers and coat, ski hat and gloves. The branches of the old oaks creak and clack in the frozen silence, complaining about winter.

Later, in bed, sleepy, you put the catalogs on the night-stand and turn out the light and listen to the wind pounding the north corner of the house, whiffling around the window frame, and you pull the heavy woolen blankets closer around you and close your eyes while wind waves surge against the house in the night and tulips, luscious as lollipops, dance in your dreams.

❊    ❊    ❊

JUST AS MONET'S WATER GARDEN kept revealing more and more to him, so garden strolls at different times of day, from different directions, in different weather, in all the seasons, will supply an endless reservoir of ideas and insights, not only on what needs to be done but what the garden can be.

After a few years of false starts and failed efforts and occasional successes, your garden notebook can help you orchestrate a garden display that extends for three seasons and capitalizes on the strengths of your property. Thereafter, the gardener may begin to move closer to perfection, to creating a memorable one-of-a-kind garden.

Once a garden becomes your own—that is, once it begins to capture a vision that is uniquely yours—it's amazing how little effort maintains it. Maybe that's because a bit of work here and a bit there, on a regular basis, really does add up; or maybe it's because, doing what you want to be doing, you lose track of time; or maybe it's because once you get to know a garden, you know what to look for and can anticipate what should be done.

Of course, every gardener loves to tinker and experiment, to try out new ideas, to keep changing, so a garden will always be a work in progress, ready to absorb as much time as the gardener wants to devote to it.

Attorney, author, avid gardener: Arthur T. Vanderbilt II practices law in New Jersey and is the author of many works of nonfiction, including *Fortune's Children: The Fall of the House of Vanderbilt, Golden Days: Memories of a Golden Retriever,* and *The Making of a Bestseller: From Author to Reader.* He has been developing the gardens around his suburban home for over twenty years.